MARCO ⊕ POLO

Travel with Insider Tips

FUERTEVENTURA

ATLANTIC
OCEAN

Azores (Port.)

Madeira (Port.)

Canary Islands
(Spain)   Fuerteventura

Western
Sahara

D1355063

www.marco-polo.com

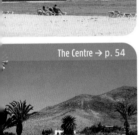
SYMBOLS

INSIDER TIP	Insider Tip
★	Highlight
●●●●	Best of ...
⛰	Scenic view
🌱	Responsible travel: fair trade principles and the environment respected

PRICE CATEGORIES HOTELS

Expensive over 450 euros

Moderate 280–450 euros

Budget under 280 euros

Average price for one week per person including half board in the cheapest room (two persons sharing)

PRICE CATEGORIES RESTAURANTS

Expensive over 12 euros

Moderate 8.50–12 euros

Budget under 8.50 euros

The prices are for a main dish without drinks

On the cover: Off-road adventure in the Wild West p. 93 | Close to the wind p. 99

CONTENTS

The South → p. 70

Trips & Tours → p. 90

Sports & Activities → p. 96

Road atlas → p. 120

DID YOU KNOW?

MAPS IN THE GUIDEBOOK

(122 A1) Page numbers and coordinates refer to the road atlas
(0) Site/address located off the map. Coordinates are also given for places that are not marked on the road atlas

**INSIDE BACK COVER:
PULL-OUT MAP →**

PULL-OUT MAP 📖

(📖 A–B 2–3) Refers to the removable pull-out map

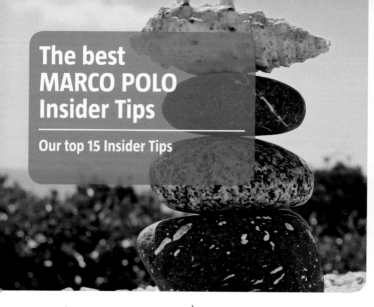

The best MARCO POLO Insider Tips

Our top 15 Insider Tips

INSIDER TIP **Big reputation**

Their reputation is as large as the Marabou stork after which it is named – the *Marabú* in Esquinzo, here you can dine inside or outdoors under the palm trees – and the ingredients are sourced locally from the island's farmers → p. 80

INSIDER TIP **Feast followed by sleep**

You know the problem: good food deserves good wine, but who does the driving back to the hotel? The *El Patio de Lajares* is the ideal solution: a gourmet restaurant with guestrooms → p. 43

INSIDER TIP **Become an artist!**

Hundreds or maybe thousands have helped to build the *pebble cairns* in Punta de Tostón. There are still more than enough pebbles lying around. All you need is a steady hand, patience and caution: one wrong move and you will have to start all over again (photo above) → p. 43

INSIDER TIP **Turtle soup**

Not to eat, but to listen to – the reggae and ska band *Sopa de Tortuga* is just one of many that form part of the music scene in Morro Jable and Jandía Playa → p. 85

INSIDER TIP **Latin rhythms**

If you really feel like dancing, it is best to go to the island's capital, *Puerto del Rosario*, where things really get going on weekends late into the night → p. 50

INSIDER TIP **Island cuisine**

A first of its kind on the island, *Casa Santa María* restaurant is beautifully decorated in the local style and since opening their doors they have become a worthy benchmark for culinary style in Betancuria (photo right) → p. 59

INSIDER TIP **Parrot fun**

The *Oasis Park* at La Lajita offers lots of animal shows, safaris, fun and entertainment and the parrot show is very funny → p. 69

INSIDER TIP **Divine dining**

There is no better place to spend a balmy summer's evening than outdoors on El Divino's sheltered terrace. The atmosphere is wonderfully romantic and the food quite 'heavenly' → p. 73, p. 75

INSIDER TIP **Wild West**

The west coast is wild and uninhabited and there is no better way to experience it than on horseback. The stables at La Pared will take you on an adventure ride → p. 78

INSIDER TIP **Dive under water!**

If you want to experience the variety of the underwater world – without getting wet – take a trip on one of the dive boats for a nautical excursion under the sea → p. 102

INSIDER TIP **Island Art**

The re-opened exhibition centre, the Centro de Arte Canario, in La Oliva presents artworks by well known local artists and sculptors → p. 44

INSIDER TIP **Pirate attack**

In the past Fuerteventura's farmers used to fall victim to pirate attacks but on occasion they were the victors – and now the beautiful Fiesta of Tuineje commemorates the event → p. 105

INSIDER TIP **A cycle up hill and down dale**

Cycling on the island is a must and a good option for bicycle rentals and organised tours is Easy Riders in Corralejo → p. 37

INSIDER TIP **Take the easy option**

A unique way to experience the island is by trike – but the motorbike variety – Fuerte Trike in Morro Jable makes it possible → p. 84

INSIDER TIP **Camel safari**

You may not actually be heading out into the desert but the 30 minute ride on the back of a camel is a lot of fun. The camel caravan starts at Oasis Park at La Lajita → p. 103

BEST OF ...

FOR FREE

● *Magnificent landscape*

How wonderful it is that the best of Fuerteventura is still free: the sand, the dunes and the ocean. Nowhere else do colours and shapes lift the spirits as much as here, in the *shifting dunes of Corralejo* → p. 34

● *Visit the past*

Even the drive through the Malpaís Grande – an uninhabitable lava field – is something special. Get a glimpse into the uncomplicated and simple lives of the island's original inhabitants when you visit the ruins of the partially restored lava huts in of the *lavascape at Atalayita* → p. 57

● *Breathtaking view*

The best lookout point on the whole island is from *Mirador Morro Velosa*. From the slopes of the 645m/2116ft high Tegú Mountain you will have a panoramic views over the island's northern valleys all the way to its volcanoes (photo) → p. 59

● *Open air art*

The *Parque Escultórico* (a sculpture park) covers the whole of the island's capital Puerto del Rosario. Some of the sculptures are permanent, while other temporary displays can be discovered when you go for a walk along the shore north of the harbour → p. 48

● *Lagoon magic*

The north has white shifting dunes, the south has the maritime lagoon landscape of the Playas de Sotavento – ideal for long walks on the endless beach, swimming, surfing or even just lazing around on the *Playa Barca* → p. 79

● *The Wild West coast*

You can experience the spray of the surf at many places along the coast but in the little fishing village of *Puertito de los Molinos* there also a beach and a duck pond giving it a feel of rural Fuerteventura on a small scale – a type of outdoor museum but without the entrance fee! → p. 92

●●●● Dots in guidebook refer to 'Best of ...' tips

ONLY IN FUERTEVENTURA
Unique experiences

● **Wind, waves, World Cup**
The island holiday experience does not get better than this: when the best *windsurfers* in the world visit the beautiful lagoon landscape of the Canary Islands they showcase their artistic skills and amaze the crowds → p. 105

● **More than just a hint of Rio**
The magnificent and impressive *Puerto del Rosario carnival* procession clearly shows what an influence South America has had on the carnival culture of the Canary Islands → p. 104

● **Expert hikes**
The countryside may look desolate but it hides a wealth of interesting and wonderful things – large and small – you just have to know where to look which is why it is best to take a hike *guided by an expert* → p. 98

● **Mansion for connoisseurs**
The *Era de la Corte* on the outskirts of Antigua is just one of many inns that have been authentically refurbished in the charming and traditional style of the old Fuerteventura – but with all the modern amenities → p. 56

● **Living history**
The large and beautifully done outdoor museum *La Alcogida* recreates a typical village from Fuerteventura's past (photo). The village comes to life with daily demonstrations e.g. bread baking in the traditional style → p. 53, p. 102

● **Authentic flair**
Betancuria, a small atmospheric town in the interior of the island, has the most beautiful shops for authentic handicrafts and some rarely visited monastery ruins, providing insight into the way life once was on Fuerteventura → p. 58

● **Endless beaches**
Located above deserted beaches that seem to go on for ever, *Cofete* gives a hint of what it used to look like on the other side of the peninsula in the 1960s before the arrival of tourism and its large hotels. Of course, there is also the mysterious Villa Winter … → p. 89

ONLY IN

BEST OF ...

● *Sights and sound*

Betancuria's *multimedia presentation* showcases the most beautiful aspects of the Canary Islands with pictures – and an accompanying sound track – that include shots of the fantastic display of flowers that appear out of nowhere after the winter rainfalls → p. 58

● *Cave adventure*

The volcanic lava cave *Cueva del Llano* is enclosed at the top and its small museum is also under cover and makes for an interesting destination when it is too hot (or too cold) for the beach (photo) → p. 39

● *Shopping trip indoors*

The multi-storied shopping centre *Las Rotondas* in the capital Puerto del Rosario offers exactly that. When it gets too hot outside its air-conditioned interior is a welcome refuge from the scorching heat → p. 49

● *Art for a change*

Finished your shopping in Las Rotondas? Then have a look at what current contemporary art Puerto del Rosario has to offer at the *Centro de Arte Juan Ismaël* – where there is also a cafeteria → p. 48

● *A poet's choice*

Still in Puerto del Rosario and this time it is a tour of the *Museo Unamuno*, the former hotel where the Spanish poet Miguel de Unamuno stayed – it is interesting enough to visit more than once – a fascinating journey into the past → p. 48

● *Dine with a view*

On the terrace of the *Mirador de Sotavento* you can dine outside, comfortably sheltered from the wind and enjoy a great view – a special combination because it is not often that you can do so → p. 79

HEAT

RELAX AND CHILL OUT
Take it easy and spoil yourself

● *Wellbeing – with chocolate and wine*
Every good hotel offers their own wellness programme with treatments (algae baths, chocolate therapy, wine massages etc.) but the *Gran Hotel Atlantis Bahia Real* in Corralejo and the *Barceló Fuerteventura Thalasso Spa* in Caleta de Fustes really do set the bar very high → p. 39, p. 62

● *Beach club atmosphere*
La Sirena bar in Corralejo offers just that: guests can stretch out on sun loungers, order a salad or cocktail and relax and daydream with their feet in the sand – the perfect way to spend the day → p. 35

● *Take to the seas*
Sailing along on a *catamaran* from Morro Jable is a real joy – no engine noise and lots of space on deck to stretch out, relax and enjoy the sea and the sail (photo below) → p. 84

● *Cocktails and live music*
The *Cervezería Olimpo* on Jandía Playa offers both, along with comfortable seating and of course you can sit outside and watch the world go by – a really relaxing way to pass the time → p. 84

● *Chill out in the capital*
Sip some excellent wine, enjoy some delicious food and take in the fresh sea air and there is no better place in Puerto del Rosario for this than the *Terraza del Muelle* → p. 49

● *Holiday within a holiday*
Gran Tarajal itself is not really a tourist highlight, but the tourist-free (well, almost) *beach promenade* has something timeless and magical about it which makes you forget everything → p. 65

● *Cocktails, cushions, patio*
Everything about the small, quaint *Café Blanco* in Corralejo is relaxing and pleasing – tasty food, comfy cushions and refreshing cocktails – they all help to transform the holiday dream into a reality → p. 38

INTRODUCTION

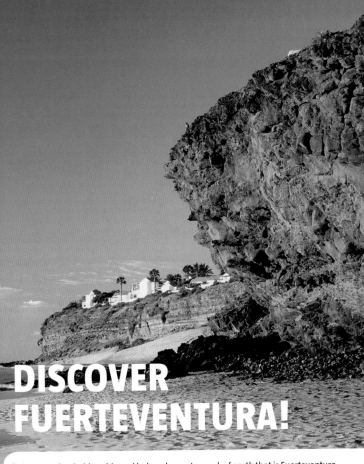

DISCOVER FUERTEVENTURA!

'It is a wasteland, this noble and beloved remote speck of earth that is Fuerteventura – an island which was once called the blessed ... a naked, bare, barren land of bones, a country which hardens a tired soul'. These are the words written by the poet Miguel de Unamuno to describe his new home. He arrived in Fuerteventura in 1924 but not as a tourist in need of a holiday, but rather as a political exile, banished from Spain to its poorest wilderness.

'An oasis in the middle of civilisation's desert,' is what he defiantly called his involuntary exile, and all the sun worshippers and surfing enthusiasts who now flock to Fuerteventura also appreciate this about the island: its primitive nature, its wild landscape of sand, stone and shrubs and its remote location the middle of the ocean. It is an island that is an austere symphony of colours: white beaches, blue skies, azure waters, parchment grassy plains and gunmetal boulders. You will find no hint of the

Photo: Beach on the Jandía peninsula

For the recluse: Ermita de la Peña in the Barranco de las Peñitas

lush vegetation of La Palmas or the scenic diversity of Tenerife, nothing of the bustling city life of Gran Canaria. Fuerteventura remains one of the most sparsely populated of the Canary islands with only a few villages and a very low population density, and the capital, Puerte del Rosario, is a small town of only 37,000 residents.

Lush green oasis in the harsh wilderness

Certain things have changed from Unamuno's time on the island: the most important is of course that tourists have arrived. The bungalows and hotel complexes of the holiday resorts are dotted like artificial oases along the island's sloped terraces, surrounded by lush landscaped gardens that would wither and die without irrigation. The resorts and hotels themselves have all the home comforts of showers, discos, bars and boutiques. But when

From the 3rd century BC
Settlement of the Canaries in at least two major waves

1st/2nd century AD
First written reference of the Canary Islands by Pliny the Elder

1403–05
The Norman, Jean de Béthencourt, conquers Fuerteventura for the Spanish Crown and establishes Betancuria

From the end of the 15th century
The Spanish Crown sends noblemen and priests who reign as señores over the locals: immigration of Norman and Spanish settlers; assimilation of the indigenous Majoreros

you step out on to your balcony nothing is like it is at home. Instead there is a world of natural and stark beauty: all you will see is sand, intense sky and ocean, and all you will hear is the sound of the constant sigh of the wind.

Naturally the hotels provide a variety of activities designed to cater to all tastes, but the island is also popular with those who seek a break from the usual sensory overload. Here, the stress of sightseeing will not put a damper your relaxation as there are neither ancient walls nor famous museums. But you should still take some time out to go on a trip or a guided hike to discover for yourself some of the island's hidden attractions – be it gorges or, the lunar landscape of the lava fields or village churches – so that you can experience the spirit of the island. How about a siesta in a small fishing or mountain village? Because in the older villages one thing reigns supreme above all: peace. There you can sit underneath a canopy of leaves in front of the village church and enjoy the hibiscus blossoms, the sunlight as it dapples the pavement and feel as though all around you time is standing still. You can even lie on the wonderful shifting dunes of Corralejo and watch the sand as it is swirled around by the wind. Or watch as the setting sun washes the landscape in light hues: the hillside in wisps of rusty reds and pale greens and the gray-green lichen on the black lava rocks. The shadows move and almost nothing happens, but yet you get the feeling that you have experienced something great.

The happiest tourists on the island are those who love water sports. But the expansive white sandy beaches and the fine weather are ideal for all kinds of activities and all levels of difficulty. The beaches at-

> **Surf Mecca in the middle of the Atlantic**

tract a colourful array of people and when competitions are announced they travel here from all over the world. Beginners can learn very quickly, as it seldom rains and there are no storms or sudden downpours. If the art of surfing doesn't appeal then one can always sail on a catamaran or try one's luck with some deep-sea fishing. The true quality of Fuerteventura is really experienced when one goes snorkelling or scuba diving; it has the most fantastic underwater-world and a plethora of dive sites along its coasts. Every diving school has their own special site. Sometimes they can be quite bizarre – like the undersea solidified lava rivers – or just clear white sand or even some old shipwrecks, teeming with fish and other sea life.

17th/18th century
Pirates repeatedly raid the coastal towns

1730–36
After a volcanic eruption residents from Lanzarote flee to the neighbouring island of Fuerteventura

1740
Citizens of Tuineje send English pirates fleeing (Tamacite)

1837
The island's *Señorío* feudal system is abolished

1852
The Canaries become a free trading zone; a boom ensues due to the export of dye, soda ash and lime

The landscape does not vary a lot: there are some volcanic peaks and deep valleys, the occasional oasis, a handful of small picturesque mountain villages, a few sleepy fishing villages and here and there a modern wind turbine or a few old windmills. The coasts on the other hand are beautiful and varied. There are the endless stretches of bright fine sandy beaches of the Jandía peninsula, the pristine white dune beaches at Corralejo, the dark almost black pebbles of the small coves of the fishing villages in the south of Maxorata while in the west wild waves buffet cliffs with narrow crags and stretches with black or golden yellow sands. Even the surf is different: on one beach little children can swim safely, on the next you have to fight strong winds and on the third, the strong current can tear you away if you venture too far out into the surf.

Travellers who like educational holidays might not be very happy with Fuerteventura. For them the most interesting aspects would be the rural lifestyle of the earlier (and even the current) islanders and just how innovative they had to be with water catchment and how they had to manage and cultivate their limited resources – all quite fascinating. Also, it must have been very difficult just to survive on this fertile, yet

Creative survival techniques

inhospitable island. Immigrants from the south of Spain and France brought new agricultural and animal husbandry methods to Fuerteventura, donkeys and camels were used for livestock breeding and transporting water from wells. The *señores* had the say then, and over the centuries life became increasingly difficult for the indigenous islanders, the *Majoreros*. At that time there were only about 6000 to 8000 residents on the island. If the rain stayed away for long periods or if locusts invaded from the Sahara, famine was inevitable. Only the *señores* and the military were eligible for aid from the outside. The military was stationed in the only commando centre, the Casa de los Coroneles in La Oliva, which today is the most important building on the island.

This impressive building – along with some old farmhouses and barns – have all been restored to their original form in recent years, and were either converted into museums, or into holiday homes. The island buzzword is 'rural tourism' especially for those tourists who would rather be armed with their reading glasses and a good book, than with scuba gear. Aside from these small inns, that are ideal for guests who do not mind the distance to the beach, tourists also stay in hotels and apartment complexes that

1912
The islands are granted self-governance

1927
Fuerteventura becomes part of the new province of Gran Canaria

1966/67
Tourism arrives

1986
Spain joins the EU; the Canary Islands obtain special status

1993
The Canaries are fully integrated into the EU

2008
Reaches the 100,000 citizens mark

seldom have less than 100 units and that are always situated close to the sea. Away from the beaches, in the interior, you are more likely to experience the authentic Spanish nature of the island, hopefully during a fiesta. This is when bands play in the town square; there are stalls selling snacks and young and old alike take to the dance floor. On the main holy day a procession moves through the village, the dignitaries in front followed by the village folk in their full festive dress. These fiestas differ from the fiestas in the fishing villages in so far as there are no boat processions. But the party does not stop with fiestas and carnival. Nowadays the traditional dates are overshadowed by new tourist draw cards – the large international events which for many are reason alone to travel. This is especially true for the annual Windsurfing World Championships and in particular, the freestyle surfers whose acrobatic antics attract a lot of spectators. In March, music enthusiasts flock to Corralejo to the Blues Festival, and in early November during the International Kite Festival the heavens above the shifting sand dunes are filled with imaginative and colourful kites.

Festival de Santo Domingo

Fortunately in this respect some variety is offered. Guided bicycle tours and hikes with varying grades of difficulty are the most accessible to do. More exciting are the motorbike or quad bike tours and if you want to learn more about the island, you will find some excellent museums, art exhibitions and galleries. At the very least you should take a daily walk on the beach, because there is no better way to restore your soul, spirit and body by striding out on the sand listening to the music of the wind and the waves. And when the last evening approaches, how to say

Processions, surfers and kites

goodbye? Another beach party? A paella with fresh seafood in the hotel restaurant? Drink sangria at the pool bar? Perhaps it would be a good idea to take one last drive to one of the sleepy fishing villages, where, on the beach terrace of one of the small restaurants you can enjoy some delicious fresh fish, drink some chilled local wine and listen to the sound of the breaking waves and feel the wind tug at your hair …

WHAT'S HOT

1 Good Morning Fuerte!

A good start In most countries, breakfast is seen is the ideal start to the day, but in Spain the *desayuno* has been rather neglected however, this is slowly but surely changing – partially thanks to the island's immigrants. There is always more than just *café solo* on offer at *Café Finny (Cosmo Shopping Center, Morro Jable)* and in *Café Colonia* you can enjoy a selection of breads and omelettes *(Edificio Esmeralda, Solana Matorral, Playa de Jandía)*. And the island now also has a master confectioner, Susan Merbold *(Cafeteria El Molina)* who bakes a selection of mouth-watering pastries and cakes *(C. Risco Blanco, Costa Calma)*.

2 Recycled Art

Sustainable art Recycle artists collect what others throw away, and then use it to create something new – and in so doing also help to keep the environment clean. João, Luis and Xandi alias *Skeleton Sea* make fish artworks from scrap metal *(www.skeletonsea.com, photo)*. The mosaic artist Angelika Heckhausen uses scrap plastic to create art, which she sells in the shops of *Clean Ocean Project*. They have shops in Corralejo, Cotillo and Lajares and also organise beach clean-ups *(www.cleanocean project.org)*.

3 Island Blues

Musical Corralejo Every year in March blues music takes over Corralejo with the start of the *Blues Festival*. Bands play in bars or outdoors under the stars like they do at the *Plaza Patricio Calero*. The *Rock Island Bar (Crucero Baleares 8)* has live music every evening and at the *Imagine Music Bar (C. Lepanto 7)* the blues are belted out regularly.

There are a lot of things to discover in Fuerteventura. A few of the most interesting are listed below

Romantically rural

4

Casas Rurales Small, boutique hotels are the exception on Fuerteventura however, a number of establishments have joined forces with the *Casas Rurales* programme offering rural cottages with an eco-tourism slant. Tinín Martínez and Zaragoza Estévez manage *Mahoh Villaverde*, a hotel and a group (by the same name) promoting the protection of the island. Their guests sleep in rustic rooms in a farmhouse dating back to the 19th century *(C. Francisco Bordón Méndez 1, Villaverde)* while the *Casa Tamasite* has old wood beam ceilings and antiques *(C. Tamasite 9, Tuineje)*. In the past animals were kept in the *Casa de la Burra* (which dates back to the 14th century) but today the charming *finca* makes use of modern technology, in the form of solar energy and water treatment plants *(Los Llanos de la Concepción, photo)*.

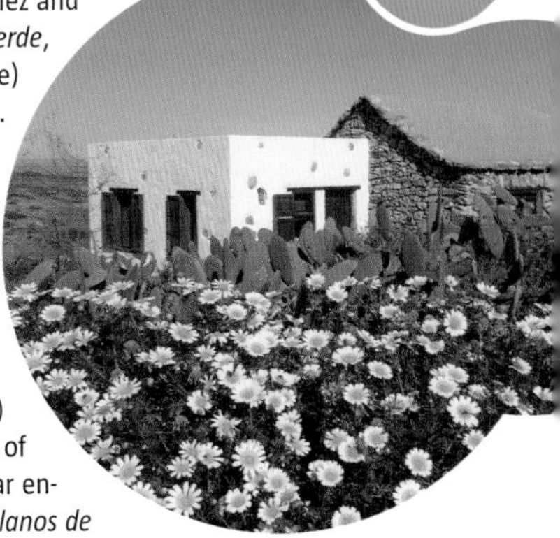

New National Sport

5

Pádel Padel tennis, or just Pádel, is a racquet sport like tennis but with smaller racquets and slower balls. The sport is very popular in Spain and of course Fuerteventura has followed the trend and there are regular competitions on the island. *Go Go Padel* is an annual tournament between Fuerteventura, Lanzarote, Gran Canaria, Tenerife, La Palma and La Gomera *(www.dgeventos.com/gogopadel)*. In 2010 it took place in the *Kapalu Urban Sports Center Mariano Barbacid (Puerto del Rosario)*. Diego di Noto from the *Academia de tenis y pádel Drop Shot* shows players how to go from beginners to pros *(www.dropshotfuerteventura.com)*. It can be played at almost any hotel, e.g. in the *Origo Mare* at Corralejo.

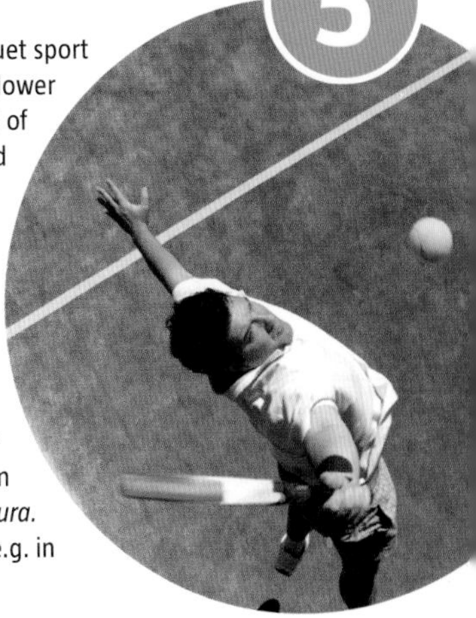

IN A NUTSHELL

BARRANCOS

When the few rainstorms occur during the winter, rushing flood waters carve deep gullies into the slopes forming ravines or *barrancos*. Some eventually form valleys or canyons. Do not miss out on the canyon-like Barrancos de Esquinzo, de los Molinos and de las Peñitas on the west coast and the Barranco de la Torre on the east coast.

CLIMATE

The ocean and trade winds mean that the island's climate is pleasant and fair throughout the entire year. The sea keeps the temperatures even and the trade winds keep away both the rain clouds as well as hot dry air masses and this is why the weather here is normally very different from that of the nearby Sahara. Only the drought is the same, and this is in contrast to the western islands of Gran Canaria and Tenerife, where the precipitation from the trade winds brings rain to the high mountains.

Fuerteventura's weather can also be somewhat fickle. Winter rainfall occurs when the trade winds move far south causing low pressure systems from the north and the west. This causes uncomfortably cool days. On other days when the hot dusty Sahara winds (Sirocco) blow

Photo: Mountain landscape in the interior

Some interesting facts about Fuerteventura: the people, the flora and fauna, nature conservation and energy production

over the island, the temperatures can rise by ten degrees or more. The trade winds blow the strongest during summer and blasts of sand mean that spending time at the beach is impossible, especially with small children.

E CONOMY

Fuerteventura was once considered the breadbasket of the Canaries but today most of its fields lie fallow. Even the hardy goats are no longer profitable enough. Fishing is only done with small boats and the catch is only sufficient for the island itself. Tomato plantations, aloe vera cultivation (in the south) and sea salt production are the only produce of any economic significance. Tourism developed relatively slowly in Fuerteventura and as late as 1968, only 1400 foreign visitors had vis-

The dusky perch in its element

ited the island, today there are almost 1.5 million tourists annually. Almost the entire island's economy is now dependent on tourism.

FAUNA
Few four-legged animals live on the island or are kept as livestock, and the most noticeable of them are the stray cats and goats that roam freely all over the island. The island's Arabian camels, which were once very important as riding and work animals, are now mainly tourist attractions. Amongst the island's wild animals, the most common are lizards, rabbits and hedgehogs. Occasionally ground squirrels can also be seen, they have been on the island since 1972 when a miner brought a pair over from the Sahara, but they escaped and began breeding. Birdlife on the island is very diverse and there are numerous birds of prey like ravens and white vultures and of course seabirds and seagulls. On the tranquil beaches the busy Sanderlings rush along the edge of the surf looking for food while the hoopoes make their nests in the valleys of the west and the rare Hubara Bustards live in the dunes of the north. When there is an increase in the rainfall, the partridges flourish. The rather nondescript wild canary can be found here in its natural habitat.

The sea around the Canary Islands is very rich in marine life and the coastal waters teem with several bass species, mackerel, plaice, eels, rays, dogfish, blue shark, sole, swordfish, tuna and squid. During spring the jellyfish arrive – especially in the waters on the west and the south – and a sting from one of their long tentacles can cause some unpleasant burning and in some cases even paralysis.

FLORA
Typical of the semi-desert vegetation of the island is its low scrubland, wild grasses, lichens and aromatic herbs and other wild flowers. Plants that have adapted to the drought are the rosette-like succulents, the spiky Euphorbia bush, as well as the agave plants which were brought in from Central America and used for the production of sisal. The prickly

pear cactus was imported from America and this plant is the host to the cochineal beetle from which red dye is obtained. Since the development of chemical colours, the need for cochineals had declined dramatically. The only indigenous tree, the Canary palm, grows in the island's oases while tamarisks grow in those ravines that have water flowing throughout the year. In February, the yellow blossoms of the mimosa bushes announce the coming of spring. In agriculture, tomato and aloe vera cultivation play the main role whilst the cultivation of grains, potatoes and vegetables has sharply decreased. Recent investigations are underway to see whether the indigenous desert truffle can be farmed on a large scale. The mushroom – which grows entirely underground and lives in symbiosis with the yellow flowering Canary Island sun or rock rose – forms its truffle bulbs after the winter rainfall.

GEOGRAPHY AND GEOLOGY

With a surface of 656mi², Fuerteventura is the second largest of the Canary Islands. It is closer to Africa than the other islands of the archipelago (shortest distance about 95km/59 mi). Delhi and Florida are on the same latitude. Fuerteventura stretches almost 98km/60mi from its northern cape, Punta de la Tiñota to the south-western cape, Punta de Jandía. Geographically it consists of the island body of Maxorata (after which the indigenous Majoreros were named) and the Jandía peninsula in the south.

Fuerteventura is the oldest of the Canary Islands and was created when the seabed rose up. The largest part of the island was formed almost 12–22 million years ago and has therefore been more affected by erosion than the younger islands. The volcanic activity only started later with the last volcanic activity happening about 4000 years ago. The dark sand and pebble beaches consist of ground lava rock, whilst the white and golden yellow sandy beaches and dunes developed from the calcification of marine animals and not – as it is often claimed – from sand blown over from the Sahara.

LUCHA CANARIA

Canarian wrestling has been practised since pre-Spanish times. Wrestlers *(luchadores)* from two 12-man teams take each other on. They have to wrestle for a maximum of three rounds of three minutes each. The loser is the wrestler who touches the ground more than twice with any body part apart from his feet. The wrestling ring is about 10m/32ft in diameter and covered with sand or sawdust. Many villages have their own arenas and tournaments are held at all festive events. The real champions are those who master all the 43 possible grips. They are treated like celebrities just the way football stars are treated elsewhere.

NATURE CONSERVANCY

Fuerteventura is characterised by drought and has an eco-system that is very sensitive to human influences and sustainability. Firstly because the plants grow very slowly in the harsh conditions and secondly, the hard dry earth also makes it difficult for plants to take root. For centuries the water consumption has exceeded the water supplied by rainfall. This has resulted in the steady decrease of groundwater levels and increased desertification. A dramatic increase in ecological stress was brought on by tourism and the impact of intensive tomato cultivation with its high water consumption. The greatest damage to vegetation however, is caused by the goats, there are just too many to be ecologically sustainable.

The first nature reserve on the island was established in 1982. It includes the shifting dunes at Corralejo as well as the island of Lobos. Since then a large area around Betancuria has been placed under protection and almost the whole peninsula of Jandía has been declared a nature reserve and large areas have been fenced off to keep out goats and off-road vehicles. Overall though, most of the conservation measures seem just to be on paper and in reality are practiced only half-heartedly. However, strict measures have been taken against off-road and cross-country driving.

In 2009, Unesco declared the whole of Fuerteventura (as well as the surrounding ocean) a Biosphere Reserve, a status that Fuerteventura is justifiably very proud of. A clear expression of their new environmental protection attempts is their ambitious project to reintroduce the loggerhead turtle back into its natural habitat. The project also takes the eggs to the beach where they then hatch naturally in the warmth of sun.

POPULATION

Fuerteventura is the most sparsely populated of the Canary Islands. In 1940, there were no more than 14,000 people on the island. The barren land and shortage of fresh water resources would just not sustain more people and it was only with the development of tourism and the subsequent building of seawater desalination plants that the population started to grow. Today the population is just over 100,000 and more than a third of them live in the capital. The native islanders, the Majoreros, never reached these numbers and today the majority of islanders come from the Spanish mainland or from the other Canary Islands. The Majoreros in turn, trace their origins to at least three different nations. In the 15th century the

island belonged to the kingdom of Spain, then the Normans who settled here after the arrival of the conqueror Jean de Béthencourt and last, but not least, the native Canarians who lived here before their surrender to the Spanish and Normans.

VILLA WINTER

No other person on the Canary Islands – certainly not during the 20th century – has ever given rise to as many myths and legends as the former landlord of the Jandía peninsula and the owner of the mysterious Villa Winter, Gustav Winter. Born in 1893 in Germany (he died in 1971 in Las Palmas) he came to Gran Canaria in 1926 as an engineer to build a power plant. In 1937 he leased the entire Jandía peninsula and built a villa. Rumours suggest that the villa had something to do with the German Reich setting up a naval base and airport in the Canary Islands. This idea never came into being, mainly because General Franco ordered Spain's neutrality during World War II and by that time Winter was no longer in the Canaries. The real era of rumour and myths around Winter began after 1946, when he returned and the peninsula was turned into an agricultural operation (especially tomato crops and livestock) and the inhabitants were apparently treated like serfs. Winter never actually lived in the mysterious and heavily guarded villa near Cofete.

WATER

There is a real water shortage on the island. It seldom rains and when it does, most of the water runs straight off into the sea. Even before the introduction of water pumping windmills (imported from the USA in the 19th century), when the water table was not that low it was necessary for the locals to be prudent

Typical island farmstead with white-washed buildings and water pump windmill

with their precious water resources. Fields were terraced and water collection tanks were installed on the slopes and domestic cisterns built. The water collected in the cisterns still had to be processed so that it could be drinkable and the limestone filtration ponds that were built can still be seen in some of the island's museums. Groundwater was hauled (and still is) from brick wells *(pozos)*, either by windmills or by animals turning the capstan wheel. This water is also stored in enclosed reservoirs but is mostly used for irrigation or as drinking water for livestock. Today, because of tourism, the increased water need is met by the desalination of seawater. Not all homes on the island are connected to the mains and many still have their drinking water delivered by a tanker.

WIND AND SOLAR ENERGY

The island has massive potential for the generation of sustainable energy by means wind and or solar power, yet neither form have been fully exploited on the island. The biggest advances have been in harnessing the trade wind with a wind farm in the north of the peninsula Jandía generating all the power required to meet the energy needs of the north island as well as the seawater desalination plant in Corralejo. Solar panel water heating is still in its infancy though as is solar power generation. Building started on a 1.4 megawatt plant in 2009 and only when the word gets out how quickly such investments can pay off here, will the pace of innovation in Fuerteventura take off.

WINDMILLS

All the brick mills are flour mills. The sails, four or six of them, are covered with canvas and although the wind usually blows from one direction only, the mills have a rotating rudder that is used so get the sails aligned into the wind. Grinding is done by hand or with an animal powering the capstan wheel, either donkeys or camels.

FOOD & DRINK

Even in the days when the island was known as the breadbasket of the Canaries, the people here were certainly not living in the land of milk and honey. Today, most of the arable land lies fallow and the only crops produced are potatoes and tomatoes.

Thanks to the EU agricultural market, the selection of produce on offer is now greater than ever – and quite international. Those who love Spanish cuisine can indulge in all the popular favourites like paella and tapas. Tapas are the tasty little appetisers – like bean salad, sardines or marinated mussels – that are served in small bowls at the bar counters in local pubs. In all the holiday resorts you will also find a range of tourist foods like pizza and pasta, bangers and mash or fish and chips and nowadays the main tourist areas even have Chinese and occasionally Greek, Mexican and Indian restaurants. But the best thing you can do is to tuck into the local dishes as potatoes and tomatoes are certainly not all the island has to offer. The menus always have a wide selection of freshly caught fish and if you stick to the local food, you will not only get fresh ingredients but also excellent value for money. Canarian cuisine may be simple and unpretentious but it also has some hearty flavours, without being too for-

Photo: Fish with *papas arrugadas*

Besides the treasure trove of fresh seafood, the island's simple cuisine also holds a few other tasty surprises

eign. There is however one prerequisite: you have to like garlic as it is used very liberally in most dishes.

A typical – and delicious – combination is fresh fish with wrinkly salted potatoes (*papas arrugadas*) and *mojo* sauce which is often also served with a small salad of tomatoes and onions. The most popular fresh fish is the *vieja* a species of the parrot fish. However *vieja* is often only availa-

ble in the better fish restaurants at the harbours. Even better (and more scarce) is fresh dusky perch (*mero*). Fresh tuna (*atún*) and squid (*calamares*) are usually always available. If you feel like ordering sole (*lenguado*), salmon (*salmón*) or langoustine (*langostas*) you should bear in mind they are imported frozen products. *Papas arrugadas* is normally served with fish but they also taste great on their own

LOCAL SPECIALITIES

▶ **Cabra/cabrito** – goat (photo above right) and kid goat meat. The latter is a seasonal dish, but goat's meat is available all year round. Kid meat dishes should be ordered a day in advance.

▶ **Cerveza** – beer and the locally brewed beers like Tropical and Dorada are to be recommended.

▶ **Gallo** – this is a fish that you will not often see on the menu. Gallo is easy to fillet and has very few (but large bones) it is special because of its firm flaky texture.

▶ **Langostinos** – large prawns that can only be eaten by getting your fingers dirty – usually served grilled and generally the most expensive dish on the menu.

▶ **Papas arrugadas** – the typical Canarian wrinkled potatoes are small unpeeled potatoes boiled in saltwater until the water has evaporated leaving the skin wrinkled and salty. They are normally served with fish dishes, but often also as a starter with a bowl of red *mojo*.

▶ **Puchero canario** – a hearty vegetable stew made with whatever garden produce is in season or available at the supermarket. Everything is put into one pot and the addition of pumpkins then gives it a smooth texture. *Pucheros* is stew with meat; the best version of this dish is served at family restaurants in the countryside.

▶ **Ron miel** – honey rum is a great after dinner drink: a glass with a measure of rum with some honey and topped off with a little whipped cream.

▶ **Sancocho** – fish dish with potatoes, sweet potatoes, onions and smoked goat's cheese.

▶ **Sopa de pescado** – fish soup that is made with as wide a variety of fish or seafood as possible – all depending on the catch of the day – served as starter.

▶ **Tapas** – this is hardly a Canarian discovery but these little appetisers are truly Spanish. People usually order a selection, for example *albóndigas* (meat balls), *patatas bravas* (fried potato cubes), *pimientos de padrón* (peppers with coarse salt), *mejillones* (mussels), *pulpo* (squid) or *tortilla* (potato omelette). If you are dining alone, two portions of *tapas* should be more than enough.

or with *mojo* sauce. The main ingredients for *mojo* sauce are garlic, red pepper, salt, vinegar and oil mixed with a variety of herbs. This makes up the red version *(mojo rojo)* the spicy red version *(mojo picón)* is made with red chillis while the green *mojo* sauce *(mojo verde)* has parsley and coriander, the green sauce tastes great with more delicate fish.

Typical fish dishes are the *sancocho* (fish with potatoes and goat's cheese) and the *sopa de pescado* (fish soup). Meat dishes are limited to goat kid *(cabrito),* mutton *(carnero)* and rabbit *(conejo)* and during the hunting season wild rabbit *(conejo salvaje)* is also available.

Goat's cheese *(queso de cabras)* is an island delicacy that is often served as a starter and when it is added to tomatoes, salami or ham it makes a delicious light lunch. The island's goat's cheese has won many awards and while it is now seldom made by hand, the form and quality of the product is still very traditional and as delicious as ever. The cheese comes in different forms of ripeness, some stronger and more aromatic, but all firm enough to cut. The firmest and most matured are *curado*.

Unfortunately the most typical of the island's dishes can no longer be found in restaurants: *gofio. Gofio* is a type of porridge which is made from grain (often barley) which is roasted, ground and the resulting flour is then made into porridge. This has been an island staple dating right back to its indigenous inhabitants, *gofio* is testimony to the poverty of the island farmers, who sometimes had to eat it (perhaps with some vegetables or goat's milk) for months on end.

Wine is mostly imported from Spain and almost always dry and Spanish brands also dominate the island's sparkling wine *(cava)* and brandy. Mineral water is always served in bottles, either *con gas* or *sin gas* – sparkling or still. An espresso or *café solo* is

a good end to a great meal. You can also order a *café con leche* (with a lot of milk) or a *cortado* (with some milk).

The local handmade goat's cheese

The differences between restaurants are negligible. They are usually not very cheap and of middling quality and only the Italian restaurants and a few gourmet establishments offer vegetarian dishes. Although service is included in the price, you may still want to add five to ten percent to the bill if you've had attentive service.

In the Canaries, as in Spain, meals are enjoyed in the afternoons and in the evenings albeit a little later than what you may be used to. Lunch *(almuerzo)* is served between 1pm–3pm and dinner *(cena)* is served from 8pm–10.30pm but in the large holiday resorts and hotels mealtimes are kept at times more suited to the foreign tourist.

SHOPPING

The Canaries are a free trading zone, but this is not something that will be felt on your pocket as the goods are not entirely duty free and transport and storage costs are high. So you may even pay more for certain items than you would back home. However, tobacco and alcohol are still very cheap. Before you buy any of the expensive products you should first compare the prices of the item with those at home!

ALOE VERA/COSMETICS

There are large plantations of aloe, the lily of the desert, on the island. The plant has well known healing properties and there is a thriving industry of aloe vera products including ointments and natural cosmetics. The products are available all over the island but do remember that goods are perishable so don't stock up too much.

ARTS & CRAFTS

One of the most popular souvenirs of the island is embroidery, and you can find out more about its history in the embroidery school in Lajares or at the *Casa Santa María* in Betancuria. The table cloths and aprons are done in a unique style that is typical to the island and really quite affordable. Another craft is the simple island pottery; locally produced pots are usually brown while white or coloured pottery is imported from the mainland. A decorative testimony to old school craftsmanship is the handicraft of the palm-leaf weavers. In the outdoor museum *La Alcogida* and in the *Molino de Antigua* you will find lovely metal and wooden objects as well as hand-made postcards.

LEATHER & SHOES

Moderately priced leather handbags, belts and backpacks are all usually imported from Morocco. There is also a wide variety of stylish Spanish shoes on offer.

LIQUOR

Brands from the Spanish mainland are very well represented and Spanish brandy is good and affordable. Craft shops sometimes also sell the local cactus liqueur and *ron miel* a rum and honey drink.

Hand embroidered items, palm-leaf basket work and natural aloe vera cosmetics are some of the local items that are still affordable

LOCAL PRODUCE

Locally produced foodstuff will last until you return home and give you a tasty reminder of your wonderful holiday. Popular items are prickly pear jam or jelly and goat's cheese; the latter is sold in four different stages of maturity, the firmest being *curado* and red cheese which is rubbed with paprika. The small round *queso de cabra* cheese wheels also keep very well. Jars of tasty mojo sauce are available in many stores. Saffron, which is generously used in the local cuisine, is worth buying here, as it is always cheaper than what you would pay for it back home.

TOBACCO

Tobacco is limited to the usual selection of well known brands as well as *palmeros*, small cigars that are rolled in La Palma.

In Corralejo and in Morro Jable you will find good Cuban wares.

WEEKLY MARKETS

There are African markets that take it in turns in Morro Jable, Costa Calma, Caleta de Fustes and Corralejo. They are popular for their sunglasses, bags and the like, also for African carvings. Remember to haggle! But do avoid buying any fake brand names as you could get into trouble with the law when you get home. A special memento of your holiday is to have your hair braided with colourful strands of pearls and beads. The ☺ farmers' market *La Biosfera* deserves special mention – it is full of local products sold directly by the supplier *(Sat 9am–2pm, upper floor of the bus station in Puerto del Rosario)*. A similar farmers' market takes place on Sundays at 9am in the *Oasis Park* in La Lajita.

THE PERFECT ROUTE

AT THE SOUTHERN TIP

We get underway in the south, at ① *Morro Jable* → p. 81. The protected salt marshes at the *Faro de Jandía*, the lighthouse at Fuerteventura's south cape, looks best when the spring tide swamps the marshes and the higher vegetations form little green islands. Now go back over Morro Jable to the third destination, the beautiful lagoon in front of ② *Playa Barca* → p. 79. From the lookout point at Risco del Paso, just south of the Playa Barca, you will get the best view over the plains – but pull off the motorway first. From here to Costa Calma the view on both sides of the road is mostly of sand: the trade winds drive the sand from the north-west coast of the peninsula across the entire country down to the south.

ACROSS THE ISTHMUS

After driving through the lush green palms of ③ *Costa Calma* → p. 72, turn left and cross the isthmus *Istmo de la Pared* – 'the wall' – in a north-westerly direction. The few inconspicuous remnants of the historic stone wall cannot be seen from the road. At ④ *La Pared* → p. 77 the landscape goes from being pale white and sandy to a darker reddish clay. There is a stop at the top of the mountain at *La Tablada* and from this vantage point you can see some wonderful views: the endless coastline stretching southwards while to the north and east, the deserted mountainous regions, home to herds of wild goats.

THE HARSH, RUGGED MOUNTAINS

In ⑤ *Pájara* → p. 65 it is time to take a break and pay a visit to the local church with its unusual Aztec-inspired facade. Then the adventurous part of the journey begins: a narrow winding road that snakes its way across the island's central mountain range. At the highest point you must stop and take in the views. Down below you will see the remains of an old dam (now flooded) that takes up the upper part of the ravine landscape of ⑥ *Barranco de las Peñitas* → p. 59. Away from the coast and tucked away in a deep and remote valley, is ⑦ *Betancuria* → p. 58, the most historically significant town on the island. Here you can easily spend two or three hours – with a visit to the church, the multi-media show in the *Casa Santa María*, shopping for prickly pear jam and handicrafts and finishing off with an afternoon snack in the most beautiful restaurant on the island.

IN THE HEART OF THE ISLAND

The trip continues downhill on the narrow winding road. The reward: a beautiful panoramic view of the north of the island. ❽ *Antigua* → p. 55, located in the broad central valley of the island, is another historic town and centre of one of the six island communities. Initially you will only pass aloe fields on the side of the road to *Pozo Negro* and later when you have turned off at the junction to the main street (FV2), you will be driving along an ancient lava river. You cross this lunar landscape on a gravel road which takes you to the ancient ruins of ❾ *Atalayita* → p. 57, the most important on Fuerteventura.

ISLAND CAPITAL AND THE SHIFTING DUNES

Now the road will take you back a little bit to a stopover at the ❿ *salt works* → p. 63 along the golf course of Caleta de Fustes, as well as the airport and further along to the island's capital ⓫ *Puerto del Rosario* → p. 47. During siesta, everything is very quiet, but you can view the *Museo Unamuno*, stroll along the harbour promenade and admire the sculptures which are dotted around the city. The last stage of the trip is towards ⓬ *Corralejo* → p. 32, with its surreal volcanic landscape that has made the north of the island famous. The main attraction though, is only reached by taking a side trip from Corralejo to the east: the dazzling white ⓭ *shifting sand dunes of El Jable* → p. 34. Since February 2012 the road to the dunes has been closed. The hotel is the furthest that vehicles are allowed: so park your car there and continue on foot.

OCÉANO

Punta de la Vera — Isla de Lobos
Punta de la Ballena o de Tostón — Corralejo ⓬ ⓭
Cotillo · Castillo de Rico Roque
ATLÁNTICO — La Oliva — FV101
Caldereta
Téfia — FV10
Embalse de los Molinos — Puerto del Rosario
Punta de los Caletones — Casillas ⓫
Bétancuria — FV20 del Ángel
Ermita de la Peña — Antigua ❽ ❼ El Matorral
Vega de Río de las Palmas ❻ Valles de Ortega — Caleta de Fuste
Fayagua — ❺ Pájara ❾ ❿
Punta de Guadalupe — Cardón — Ruinas Guanches
La Pared ❹ — FV2 — Punta de la Entallada
Costa Calma — La Pared ❷ — La Lajita — Tarajalejo — Gran Tarajal
❸ Playa Esmeralda
❶ Jandía Playa
Morro Jable

Approx. 190km/118mi, driving time approx. 5 hours. Detailed map of the route on the back cover, in the road atlas and the pull-out map

THE NORTH

Even after repeated visits to the island, it will always be an unforgettable experience: that first glimpse of the shifting dunes of El Jable. Suddenly, a white dream world opens up before you with mountains and valleys of shimmering shifting sands, as far as the eye can see. This is certainly the most impressive landscape on the whole and one sure to leave a lasting impression.

The north also has some other unusual landscapes with row upon row of extinct volcanoes lining up in beautiful symmetry. Black lava rocks are strewn over desolate areas while further south the landscape is a study in russet and red; especially when the sun catches it. Of the three large towns only Corralejo is geared towards tourism. La Oliva counts as one of the five historical towns and administers both Cotillo (which is not often visited by tourists) and Corralejo. Puerto del Rosario, the island capital, is not very touristy and is also greatly underrated as a tourist destination.

CORRALEJO

(123 E1) (*Ⅲ G2*) The main tourist attraction in the north owes its appeal to the 7.7mi² dune area of El Jable on its south-

Fascinating contrasts north-west of the island capital Puerto del Rosario: bright white sands and barren black lava

ern edge, which merges seamlessly into the beach.

Corralejo is not really the 'village' that most brochures like to call it. This town is more vibrant, diverse and international than any other town on the island. The town consists of a densely populated core which is mostly inhabited by Spanish people and a wide belt of hotels and apartment complexes that expands to the south and the east.

It has only been settled since the 19th century. In 1940, it was a small fishing village consisting of only twelve houses and when the first holiday apartments were built in 1967, the town had neither water nor electricity. This only changed during the 1970s with the start of a building boom which intensified during the 1980s. The main road and the pedestrian zone, with its many shops and restau-

Beach bar in Corralejo

are the main highlights of the island. The white sand dunes are constantly shifted by the north-east trade winds and these dunes, with their green flora valleys and rare animals, have formed their own precious ecosystem. The area was declared a protected nature reserve in 1982, but by then a part of the northern edge had already been developed. The temptation to fill the municipal coffers, by issuing building permits, was just too great for La Oliva's church fathers – Corralejo falls under the administration of La Oliva – but the biggest sin has to have been the construction of two large hotels, *Tres Islas* and *Oliva Beach,* on the most pristine part of the dunes. Although it was later proven that the buildings were constructed illegally, the owner (the hotel chain Ríu) still managed to obtain licenses for the hotels to trade: ten years for *Oliva Beach* and thirty years for *Tres Islas*. Only after the permits have expired will the hotels – which threaten the ecological equilibrium of the dunes – be allowed to be torn down. The dune area is still being threatened by simultaneous building projects on the north and in the south. Particularly worrying, from a dune ecological point of view, are the high-rise building projects in the north where the buildings are allowed to be as high as five storeys. However, there has been some small progress in the matter with the closing of the road through the dune area in February 2012. Now the sand will once again be allowed to reclaim the road. Please be aware that driving on the dunes is strictly prohibited.

rants, form the urban centre and at night a festive atmosphere reigns. There is also a promenade along the water's edge where you can enjoy a meal and something to drink. Statues on the pier honour the sailors of Corralejo who have made outstanding contributions to the development of the town during difficult times. Apart from the Playas de Sotavento in the south, the ● ★ *El Jable shifting dunes*

FOOD & DRINK

Nowhere else on the island will you find as many restaurants with sea views, as on the narrow pedestrian promenade with the rather grand name of Avenida Marítima. The *Marquesina (Moderate)* on the small pier has a solid reputation and their delicious seafood crêpes deserve a special mention. You can choose your own fish at the counter, something that the other venues in the area also offer. There are generally only small differences in the quality and prices of the restaurants, and do not expect very personal service. Heading northwards (toward the harbour) you will find El Sombrero (closed Wed | Moderate), whose speciality is meat dishes. The interior, decorated in colourful cattle hides, is a landmark in itself. A typically Spanish tapas restaurant (and one that is not often frequented by tourists) can be found behind El Sombrero: the Antiguo Café del Puerto (Budget).

It wouldn't be a real holiday unless you could have dinner with your feet in the sand. When you leave the promenade towards the south, several restaurants offer this pleasure. The best is also the first one: ● INSIDER TIP La Sirena (Moderate). Couches and loungers provide a real beach-club atmosphere, but if you prefer, you can also dine seated on proper wooden chairs. Here, and in the next two restaurants (Waikiki, Corintia), they also serve breakfast. Away from the beach, is INSIDER TIP Ambaradam where they have been serving the best coffee in town (from 8.30am) as well as crêpes, sandwiches and various pastries (CC Cactus | at the beginning of Avda. de las Grandes Playas). Secreto del Sur serves delicious ice-cream, also muesli, croissants, cakes and more (Avda. Nuestra Señora del Carmen | Duna Park, local 3).

EL ANDALUZ

Manolo and his Austrian wife Birgit are responsible for Corralejo gourmet restaurant. But be warned: there are only seven tables so you have to make reservations in advance. Smoking venue. Evenings only | closed Sun | C. La Ballena 5 | tel. 6 76 70 58 78 | Moderate

AVENIDA

Simple and unpretentious and the servings of fish are very generous. It is often very loud and crowded and has a great vibe. If you arrive after 7pm you may have to queue. Daily | C. Pizarro/corner of General Prim (close to Bristol Playa) | tel. 9 28 87 59 51 | Budget–Moderate

LA SCARPETTA

The best Italian restaurant in town. Choose from their daily specials and do not miss out on the excellent espresso! Closed Sun | CC La Menara (with the bell tower) | tel. 9 28 53 58 87 | Moderate

SHOPPING

On the main road you will find almost everything, but the prices are quite high. Dany Sport, the largest sports shop in the area, sells hiking and camping equipment, swimming and sportswear and also roller skates (Avda. Nuestra Sra. del Carmen 42). Next door in the basement, the Galería Canaria sells some useful

★ **Shifting sand dunes of El Jable**
White sand as far as the eye can see – a natural attraction of towering sand dunes that are constantly on the move
→ p. 34

★ **Outdoor museum La Alcogida**
A living museum in Tefia where you can experience how the islanders once lived and worked
→ p. 53

MARCO POLO HIGHLIGHTS

items (also toys) and various interesting knick-knacks.

La Tienda is INSIDER TIP the best tobacconist on the island that sells not only fine Havana cigars, but also some high quality alcohol, including a few bottles of extremely rare Fuerteventura wines *(C. José Segura Torres 3)*. *La Fuentita (at the beginning of the pedestrian zone)* stocks the best range of arts and crafts in the area and INSIDER TIP *Blanc du Nil* selling clothes made exclusively from Egyptian cotton in a variety of cuts and weaves *(Avda. Nuestra Señora del Carmen 62)* is not be missed. *Paradise (C. Playa Choleón, corner C. Bajo Amarillo)* specialises in surfing equipment and has everything a surfer needs. On Mondays and Fridays there is an African flea market selling belts, cheap watches, jewellery, wood carvings, tee-shirts and towels. There are also people who braid hair, and don't forget to haggle! *9am–1pm | on the main road on the Baku grounds*

SPORTS & ACTIVITIES

BAKU

What was originally planned as an ambitious and elaborate theme park now looks more like the ruins of a failed investment. Near the southern entrance is a massive capsizing galleon but aside from the flea market that takes place here on Mondays and Fridays, the only other popular attraction is the water park section with its giant waterslides and other swimming facilities. *Mid June–mid Sept daily 10am–6pm, closed Dec–mid May, otherwise Fri–Tue 10am–5pm | entrance 20 euro, after 3pm 15 euro | www.baku fuerteventura.com*

BOAT/FISHING TRIPS

Small stands along the harbour promenade sell tickets for kinds of activities like for example, a cruise on the glass-bottom boat the *Celia Cruz (1 hour 18 euro)*. Other boats can be rented for several hours for

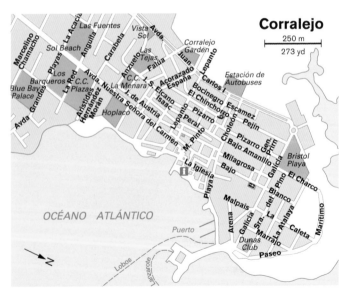

fishing trips and *Fuertevela* offer trips on a yacht *(tel. 6 19 03 68 35)*.

BICYCLES/MOTORCYCLES
In the town centre, bikes can be hired from *Vulcano Biking (C. Acorazado España 8 | tel. 9 28 53 57 06)* while organised INSIDER TIP off-road bicycle trips can be arranged through *Easy Riders (C. Las Dunas, local 2 | tel. 6 26 55 57 57 | www.easyriders-bike*

JETSKI
Due to the noise issue these watercraft can only be used during certain times. *Pier at the harbour.*

BEACHES
Playa de Corralejo does not refer to the small town beach, but the dune beach 5km/3mi further to the south-east at *Tres Islas* and *Oliva Beach hotels*. About 1.5km/

Good spot for a rest on your bicycle trip: the small village beach at Corralejo

center.com). Motorcycles and scooters are available from *Bike Point (Calle Hibisco 1, local 30 (EKZ El Campanario) | tel. 6 39 48 93 33)*. Off-road quad tours – the two-seater four-wheel drive vehicles are ideal for the desert conditions – are also very popular. *Quad Adventures (Avda. Nuestra Señora del Carmen 19 | tel. 6 60 09 96 94 | www.quadadventure.net)*.

GOLF
Tucked away at the very southern end of town is the nine hole course of Mirador de Lobos Golf. *You will need to ask for directions | tel. 6 50 65 23 35*

1mi south of the hotels, where the traffic does not pass close to the beach, is a nudist area. Take note of the signal flags: if it is red, swimming is not allowed due to strong currents and if it is yellow you exercise caution and stay close to the shore.

DIVING, SNORKELLING, SWIMMING
Spend some time exploring the underwater world of Corralejo with *Dive Center Corralejo (C. Nuestra Señora del Pino 22, close to Dunas Club | tel. 9 28 53 59 06)* or with the dive school *Punta Amanay (C. El Pulpo 5 | at the Dunas Club | tel. 6 56 44 76 57)*.

CORRALEJO

Snorkelling safaris to the small island of Los Lobos are available through *Get Wet* (tel. 6 60 77 80 53, Udo) and *Fuerte Snorkeling* (tel. 6 80 85 61 22, Veronica) and you

Swimming pool above the beach: RIU Hotel Tres Islas Pool

can take swimming and snorkelling lesson with *Swimfuerte*, for information and as a meeting point, go to *Extreme Animals & Sports* (C. las Dunas | local 3 | tel. 9 28 53 53 62).

WINDSURFING

For beginners the small bay at the local beach is the best spot and it is also where

the surf school *Ventura Surf* hires out its surfboards (tel. 9 28 86 62 95 | www. ventura-surf.com) and a short walk north of the hotel Tres Islas is the *Flag Beach Windsurf Center* (tel. 9 28 86 63 89 | www. flagbeach.com), which also offers kite-surfing.

ENTERTAINMENT

The *Plaza Felix Estévez González* in the pedestrian zone is the hub of the nightlife: popular for an evening stroll, and full of options to eat out or enjoy a drink or some live music. The discos are concentrated in the *Centro Atlántico* but they only start filling up quite late at night, usually with tourists.

SEVEN PINTS
A very well known English family bar that is conveniently situated in the centre of town. *La Plaza*

CAFÉ BLANCO ●
Lovely cocktail bar with comfortable cushions and a patio. *C. La Iglesia, corner of C. María Santana Figueroa*

ROCK CAFÉ
Popular venue for night owls – and not just for the very young – with a beautiful terrace. *No. 8 Main Road | CC Plaza*

WAIKIKI
Sip your cocktails right on the beach with sea views. Disco on Saturdays. *C. Aristides H. Morán*

WHERE TO STAY

ATLANTIC GARDEN
The 168 modern, spacious and very affordable apartments are situated next to the shopping centre, *El Campanario*, east of the town. Three swimming pools

and tennis facilities. *Avda. Gran Canaria 7 | tel. 9 28 86 71 63 | www.grandholidays club.com | Budget*

BARCELÓ CORRALEJO BAY
Four star hotel that is central, close to the beach and highly recommended. Some of the 231 rooms have sea views. Tennis courts and swimming pools (heated in winter). *Avda. de las Grandes Playas 12 | tel. 9 28 53 60 50 | www.barcelo.com | Expensive*

LA CABAÑA
Five reasonably priced apartments. In the morning the proprietor spoils her guests with freshly baked bread rolls. Direct bookings only. *C. Nuestra Señora del Pino 14 | tel. 9 28 53 50 39 | Budget (without board)*

GRAN HOTEL ATLANTIS BAHÍA REAL ●
This is the island's leading luxury hotel. Three features that stand out: its spectacular wellness area with cutting-edge cosmetic and physiotherapeutic treatments; its four elegant restaurants serving gourmet cuisine (including one Japanese) and finally; the hotel's high standard of service. Of the 242 rooms, 72 are suites are as big as 1722ft². With all that this hotel has to offer you may never want to leave! *Eastern end of the Avenida de las Grandes Playas | tel. 9 28 53 64 44 | www. atlantishotels.com | Expensive*

LAS MARISMAS
Las Marismas opened in 2003 with 232 two and three bedroom apartments and quickly gained popularity. It is situated in a quiet area (just east of Baku) and has both freshwater and saltwater pools, tennis facilities, squash courts, mini golf and good child care facilities. *C. Huriamen | tel. 9 28 53 72 28 | www.lasmarismas.info | Moderate*

RIU OLIVA BEACH/RIU TRES ISLAS
Right in the middle of the dunes and with a view of the ocean – now that is something! Building is no longer allowed in this area. The *Oliva Beach (401 rooms)* is exclusively run as a club hotel, the more expensive *Tres Islas (372 rooms)* has a beautiful garden. Both offer plenty of activities and sport. *Oliva Beach: tel. 9 28 53 53 34 | Tres Islas: tel. 9 28 53 57 00 | both www. riu.com | Expensive*

INFORMATION

OFICINA DE TURISMO
At the small pier | tel. 9 28 86 62 35

WHERE TO GO

CUEVA DEL LLANO (123 D3) *(𝄢 G3)*
For a long time it was only known to locals, now it is a popular tourist destination: at

LOW BUDGET

▶ The *Flagbeach Windsurf Center* manages the seven roomed hostel *Sol y Mar* in the centre of Corralejo. A night in a four bed room including breakfast (and lots of surf tips) will cost you 15 euro. *C. Bajo Blanco 7 | tel. 9 28 86 63 89*

▶ At the Italian self-serve restaurant, *Da Uli* in Corralejo, all the meals are under 6 euro! *C. Crucero Baleares.*

▶ Easy on the pocket: at the *Café Lounge* in Corralejo a large beer (even if you do have to get it yourself at the bar) will only cost you 2 euro and there is also free Wi-Fi. *C. Pulpo 6 (next to Dunas Club)*

● 648m/2125ft this is the largest lava cave on the island. It was formed more than a million years ago when lava flow cooled and formed a solid outer casing but continued to flow under the surface leaving a lava pipe. The resultant tube has a diameter of 7–10m/23–33ft and can be explored using mining lamps. The 300m/900ft entrance into the cave is done in complete darkness (but with a guide) and it is the main adventure, as the rest of the cave offers little of interest. Details of the geology and a unique species of blind spider (that is only found there) are displayed in a small exhibition. *Tue–Sat 10am–6pm | entrance 5 euro | 11km/7mi on the FV101 towards Villaverde, then turn right to Lajares (signposted)*

LANZAROTE
(0) (*🕮 0*)
This island, which is well known for its natural wonders, can be seen from Corralejo. Boats travel between the islands several times daily, departing from the main pier. The crossing takes about 25 minutes with the normal ferry and about 12 minutes in the large catamaran. The travel agencies on the main road will have more information about guided day trips. Detailed information can also be found in Marco Polo Travel Guide 'Lanzarote'.

LOBOS (123 E–F1) (*🕮 H1–2*)
Only 2.3mi² this small island has been a nature reserve and car-free zone since 1982. It is a lovely excursion to take a (half) day boat trip to the island for some hiking and swimming. The full name is Isla de los Lobos which means seal island, although there have not been any seals on the island for quite some time.
Close to the pier is an information centre which details the importance of the island's natural history. To the left there is a shallow swimming bay and a 127m/417ft high volcanic cone. From the main hiking paths you can walk to the lighthouse on the northern cape and back in 2–3 hours. In the tiny fishing village – turn right at the pier – you can find something to eat and drink. Take some provisions with you, especially water and remember to properly dispose of your waste in Corralejo. *Several daily crossings from 10am*

LA ROSITA
(123 D3) (*🕮 G3*)
A private farming museum with real livestock and a good shop that sells a selection of produce including jams, palm syrup and literature about the Canary Islands. The historical photos are also interesting. *On the FV 101, 9.5km/5.5mi to the south, on the right hand side (signposted) | Mon–Fri 10am–5pm, Sat 10am–3pm | entrance 5.50 euro*

COTILLO

(122 B2) (*🕮 E3*) **This sleepy fishing village in the north-west of the island is ideal for those who want to get away from it all for some peace and quiet. The village looks like Corralejo twenty years ago.**
It may just fall short of being idyllic but it does have exactly the kind of rough simplicity that many people love. Cotillo's history goes back to the 17th century, when the village served as a trading port. To protect the port, a defence tower, *Torre del Tostón,* was built in 1743 at the southern edge of the town. At the same time a sister tower, Caleta de Fustes was also built. However, by that time the era of the dreaded pirate attacks was almost over, so the old walls do not have any dramatic tales to tell. Today it houses temporary art exhibitions. The nearby lime kilns are testimony to El Cotillo's former economic importance. The old harbour was – and is – hard to

access from the sea, because an off-shore reef breaks the swell and only allows a very narrow passage. Very good nautical skills and an abundance of faith are necessary to steer through this passage and that also explains the inscription on the harbour's rock wall: *Viva la Vigen del Buen Viaje* or 'Long live the sacred Virgin of good travel'. If you arrive by car the country road

FOOD & DRINK

Seafood and fish lovers are in their element in Cotillo. During weekends people even travel from as far as Puerto del Rosario to dine in local restaurants. Particularly noteworthy is *El Mirador* at the old harbour, where you can enjoy fresh fish at sunset on the roof terrace with panorama views

Tourism is incidental here: fishing boats in the Cotillo harbour

leads you straight into the village. Turn left just before the end of the village and you will reach the tower, the lime kilns, the new harbour, various restaurants and a large beach. Turn right just before the end and you will come to the old harbour with some lovely restaurants – this is the quaintest part of Cotillo. If you would like to go to the small swimming bays and to Punta de Tostón, just follow the main road that bends sharply a few times to the right.

(closed Thu | C. Muelle de los Pescadores 19 | tel. 9 28 53 88 38 | Moderate). Even closer to the coast and the waves is *Vaca Azul*, which also has a terrace, the popular 'blue cow' has really improved lately *(daily | northern side of the old harbour | tel. 9 28 53 86 85 | Moderate)*. North of this venue is *Azzurro*, an excellent Italian restaurant that also has tables with sea views *(closed Mon | right on the road that leads to the Punta del Tostón | tel. 9 28 17 53 60 |*

Moderate). Just above the old harbour, the *Aguayre* bar and café attracts those wanting to indulge in pizzas, tapas, nachos and a sea view. The INSIDER TIP bakery *El Goloso (C. León y Castillo | at the northern edge of town)* is popular for their good coffee and delicious cakes.

BEACHES

The beach south of Cotillo gets some large surf and attracts those who prefer waters that are a little more exciting, especially the bodyboarders and surfers. The conditions are not ideal for less confident swimmers and surfers and there are also a number of flat rocks in the water at places. The small bays to the north of *Playas de los Lagos*, are protected by reefs and the water here is always calm, making them safe even for children.

WHERE TO STAY

COTILLO LAGOS
The name reveals where you will stay: right on the bay, the *Lagos de Cotillo* north of the village. For those in need of peace and quiet there are 161 studios and apartments at affordable prices. *Tel. 9 28 17 53 88 | Budget*

JUAN BENÍTEZ APARTAMENTOS
Off the main road on the southern edge of the village. This small resort has nine spacious apartments all with modern facilities and a balcony or terrace. Lovely sea views and a swimming pool. *Direct booking only | C. la Caleta 10 | tel. 9 28 53 85 03 | juanbenitez7@hotmail.com | Budget (without board)*

WHERE TO GO

LAJARES
(122 C3) (*ØD F3*)
This small hamlet is 8km/5mi from El Cotillo and is on the road between Corralejo and El Cotillo. The town is famous for its embroidery school *Natividad Hernández López* and its craft workshop Artesanía Lajares (on the right hand side in the direction of Corralejo). The workshop sells the famous embroidery as well as traditional

INVOLUNTARY EXILE

Up until the 20th century, the Canary Islands – especially Hierro and Fuerteventura – were for Spaniards what Australia once was for the British: a place where they could send criminals and insurgents. At that distance they could no longer be a nuisance. Miguel de Unamuno (1864–1936) an important Spanish poet and philosopher who immortalised Fuerteventura in his book, 'De Fuerteventura a París' was one of the men sent into exile on Fuerteventura by the Spanish government. He was exiled in 1924 because of his opposition to the military dictator Primo de Riveras. During the time of the republic, the dictator Franco also banished head of his opposition, the anarchist Buenaventura Durruti to the island. Not everyone experienced Fuerteventura as an 'oasis in the desert of civilisation' and Unamuno organised his own escape from the island. Nevertheless a monument commemorating him was erected on the island.

pottery and other arts and craft of the island. Visitors can also learn more about the development of the craft of embroidery. A popular photo opportunity in Lajares is the three-storey high *windmill* on the old road to Oliva (signpost Ermita). Diagonally across from the stone one is a second wooden windmill.

Los Pinchitos – the kebabs – is a village restaurant that is renowned for its excellent goat meat dishes *(on the right on the road to Corralejo | closed Wednesdays | Budget)*. What happens when a gourmet chef and his wife open a country guest house on the Canary Islands? INSIDER TIP *El Patio de Lajares* is the result and it has it all: a destination ideal for lovers of fine dining and French wines – with the added advantage that after your meal is over, your bed awaits in one of the six guest rooms. Reservations are necessary for meals (afternoons from 1.30pm, evenings from 7pm). *Closed Mon/Tue | on the old country road from Lajares towards Cotillo | tel. 6 50 13 40 30 | www.patio-lajares.com/uk | Expensive*

Surfers and their friends meet for salads, curries and burgers in the *U-Turn* bar (and surf shop) on the right as you exit the town towards Corralejo.

Also noticeable in the area are the man size walls of loosely stacked lava rocks. Areas of land have been enclosed in these walls made up of large lava rocks. Some of the very low walls were paved in order to catch rain water but the higher walls were built to keep the goats out of newly planted crops. These walls were not built by the farm labourers of the powerful landlords, but by goat farmers. Today the fields are no longer cultivated.

PUNTA DE TOSTÓN
(122 B1) *(⌀ E2)*

From Cotillo a cul-de-sac leads to the white sandy beaches (and a few abandoned building sites) of the *Playas de los Lagos* along to the north-western cape over 4km/2.5mi away, with lighthouses from three generations. The premises now house a *fishing museum*, which is dedicated to the traditional fishing methods of the *Majoreros (Tue–Sat 10am–6pm | entrance 3 euro)* and there is also a small cafeteria.

Punta de Tostón lighthouse

In the western foothills you can partake in the creation of INSIDER TIP land art: over the years visitors have built rock cairns from lava rocks some of which are now daring balancing acts with astounding heights. There is a track that takes you on to Corralejo. During the summer months the area is full of Spanish campers.

LA OLIVA

(123 D4) *(ᗰ F4)* **The small town in the volcanic north of the island is the centre of the traditional agricultural region.**
This is also the administrative centre for the northern part of the island. From 1709 to 1859 Oliva was the official residence of the island's governor. The town takes its name from the olive cultivation that was practised here for centuries.

CASA DE LOS CORONELES
The two-storey residence with crenulated towers and 40 rooms is the most important secular building on the island. It was built in the 17th century as a manor. At the beginning of the 18th century, after the fall of the *señores*, the military government took occupation – hence its name which means 'the colonel's house'. In November 2006 the newly renovated building was reopened by King Juan Carlos. The interior has not been restored but part of

The beautifully restored Casa de los Coroneles in Oliva looks just like a fort

SIGHTSEEING

CASA DE LA CILLA
This historic building was once an old church tithe barn and now houses a museum dedicated to the crops and agricultural tools used by the island's farming industry. It has information about the agricultural equipment used and displays of old photos that provide some insights into the island's economy. *On the road towards Cotillo | Tue–Sat 10am–6pm (sometimes closes earlier!) | entrance 1.50 euro*

the building is used for temporary art exhibitions. *Tue–Sun 10am–6pm | entrance free | at the southern edge of town*

INSIDER TIP ▶ CENTRO DE ARTE CANARIO
After being closed for a long time, this special exhibition centre was reopened in July 2010. The art centre was made possible by a private foundation and consists of an historic building, the *Casa Mané*, two underground exhibition halls and a large garden with numerous outdoor sculptures. Most of the works on display are by local con-

temporary artists. *On the southern outskirts opposite the Casa de los Coroneles | Mon–Sat 10am–5pm | entrance 4 euro*

CHURCH

The Iglesia de Nuestra Señora de la Candelaria is a white triple naved church built in 1711. It features a dark stone tower, a baroque altar of St Mary and a pulpit with effigies of the four evangelists. *No set opening times | village centre*

WHERE TO STAY

INSIDER TIP ▸ VILLA VOLCANA

On the northern slope of the volcano Monte Arena (sand mountain), west of the suburb Villaverde, is a small house with a large garden and a fantastic views. The four apartments (with terraces) have beautiful interiors and are ideal for holiday-makers seeking some peace and quiet. *Direct bookings only tel. 9 28 86 86 90 or 6 08 92 83 80 | Budget (without board)*

WHERE TO GO

TINDAYA (122 B4) *(ØD E–F4)*
After heading about 5km/3mi south-west on the main road from La Oliva you will come across *Mount Tindaya* on your right hand side. The almost 400m/1300ft high volcano which is made up of the marble-like volcanic rock (trachyte) and has a red colour due to iron oxide. The ancient residents considered the mountain sacred and left more than one hundred engravings of feet that are linked to the position of the sun in the winter, the summer solstice as well as to the position of the moon and Venus. It appears as if the summit was used as a type of observatory and also as the centre for a sun cult. The mountain was declared a natural monument in 1994. Despite the fact that its historical importance was well known, in 1991 a mining company managed to obtain the rights to use it as a quarry. Although the work was later halted, the wound that has been ripped into the mountain is a testimony to political corruption which is quite indifferent to the protection of nature and history and far more concerned about the amount of profit to be made.

The sculptor Eduardo Chillida (1924–2002) had a very controversial plan to turn the mountain into a huge work of art. Chillida wanted to transform the interior of the mountain by building a cubic shaped cave in its centre with two vertical and one

RURAL TOURISM

The busier it is along the island's coasts, the more the interior attracts those seeking some peace and quiet for hikes and relaxation. The island's government is encouraging and supporting the trend and there are now about two dozen stylish country hotels, amongst them *La Era de la Corte* in Antigua → p. 56 and the *Casa Isaítas* in Pájara → p. 66. Guided ☺ hikes → p. 98 also form part of rural tourism, as well as the museums and the re-development of the historical pathways called *caminos reales* (royal roads) that linked the old villages with each other. Learn more from Mrs von der Twer, a pioneer of rural tourism and landlady of the *Villa Volcana* → p. 45 in La Oliva. More information about the country hotels at *www.ecoturismo canarias.com*.

horizontal tunnel leading from the cave to the outside. His plan was to highlight the relationship between the mountain, the heavens and the sea in an entirely new way. The island's government ignored protests from environmentalists and con-

Fuerteventura, although he did not come to the island of his own free will. His criticism of the Spanish government resulted in him being dismissed from his position at a university and sent into exile on Fuerteventura in 1924.

Tindaya: a mountain that was regarded as holy by the island's original inhabitants

servationists and decided to go ahead with the plan. Some 11.8 million euro was spent on a feasibility study but the money just seeped away. A second study declared the plan to be feasible however a building contract has yet to be issued. Hiking up the mountain is not permitted.

A little further along the road, on the slope of Montaña Quemada (122 B4–5) (⌘ B–C5) you will see the monument to the poet, philosopher and Franco opponent, Miguel de Unamuno. He is the most famous Spanish author to write about

When you turn off to Tindaya, you can also drive on to *Playa de Jarug*, a beach on the western coast that is off the beaten track. To get there, turn right at the *Bar González*, then left at the white tower of a small substation, and right again at the following road. When you pass the last house (on the left is a large palm tree) the tarmac road leads left at a intersection on the right. At the next fork, turn right and then follow the track, at this point you will be better off if you are driving an off-road vehicle or a mountain bike. This detour is only an option if the weather is good. When swimming here it is best to stay in the shallows!

VALLEBRÓN/MIRADOR MONTAÑA DE LA MUDA (*M* F5)

East of Tindaya, a winding uphill road leads to a viewing point, the ☆ *Mirador Montaña de la Muda* (122 C5). There is a parking area with a pathway that takes you to the actual viewing platform with an explanatory panel (text in Spanish and English). From here you can view a large part of the north-west of the island, especially Mount Tindaya. If you time your arrival for the early morning, just before sunrise, you will see the intense red hues on the rocks.

Now the road heads eastward to *Vallebrón* (123 D5) a little village nestled in a valley which has escaped the impact of tourism. Here, more than anywhere else on the island, some of the traditional farming methods have remained in use. This is in a large part due to the fact that the area receives a little more rain than elsewhere. Carob and fig trees grow between the fields and the entire valley is a nature reserve.

PUERTO DEL ROSARIO

(127 E1) (*M* G–H6) **A trip to Fuerteventura is like a trip to any popular holiday club or resort area but the island's almost tourist-free capital is another world altogether and much closer to the real Spain.**

Puerto Rosario (the short form of the name) is not very old nor is it especially beautiful, yet the harbour town with 25,000 inhabitants is one of the liveliest places on the island.

From 1797 the town developed as the harbour for the nearby hamlet of Tetir. A fresh spring attracted goats and so the new settlement was called *Puerto de Cabras* (goat harbour). With the increase of maritime traffic to Gran Canaria, Tenerife and to the mainland, many Spaniards and Gran Canarians began to settle here. In 1835 the little town grew to 500 inhabitants and became a town in its own right and independent of Tetir. Its growth and development was then further increased by English merchants who shipped soda, dye (from the cochineal beetle) and lime from here. For several years Great Britain even had a consulate here.

The first boom period ended before 1990, when the natural products being exported lost their economic importance. Puerto de Cabras overtook the older towns as the most important port of the island and as the central entrance to the island, and by 1860 was considered Fuerteventura's capital. In the 1900s more and more administrative buildings went up and the first hotel opened its doors. Gradually the 'goat harbour' name seemed inappropriate and in 1956 the town was renamed Puerto del Rosario (port of the rosary) in honour of the holy Virgin of the Rosary, the patron saint of the city. The citizens were less enthusiastic though when a large part of the Spanish Foreign Legion (about 3000 men) was sent here during the mid 1970s. Crime increased dramatically and in the south of the town an infamous entertainment district, *barrio chino* (Chinatown), was established. The red light area no longer exists, the Legion was called back and the regular infantry took over the barracks.

From the 1980s onwards the overall appearance of the town has improved: historical buildings have been restored, parks and a promenade have been built and interesting sculptures placed around the public spaces. Especially attractive is the town centre with the island's administrative seat *(Cabildo Insular)*, the church and the town hall. The improvements have also resulted in tourists from passing cruise ships visiting the town, much to the delight of its citizens and the town council. Puerto del Rosario also has the added attraction of a large number of cultural activities.

Here is one option for a local sightseeing tour: from the *Parque Municipal*, south of the bus station, where the two main roads cross, turn down the main road León y Castillo. The first building on your right hand side is the wrestling arena. Behind the arena is the rectory, take the parallel road in front of the house. Further down from here you will pass the *Casa Museo Unamuno* and the church will be on your left. At the next corner you will see the *Cabildo Insular* (the island's administrative building) on your right and on the left the town hall. Further down you will reach the harbour and its promenade. From here, go back up the León y Castillo again and turn left at the town hall to reach the sizeable commercial centre which is also a pedestrian zone.

SIGHTSEEING

CASA MUSEO UNAMUNO ●
The museum is in the rooms of an old hotel where the Spanish writer and philosopher Miguel de Unamuno (1864–1936) lived for four months during his exile in 1924. Also staying with him was the journalist Rodrigo Soriano. Visitors can take a trip into the past and view his writing desk, his bed and even his chamber pot and the kitchen has been kept exactly as it was during his day. *Mon–Fri 9am–2pm | free entrance | next to the church*

CENTRO DE ARTE JUAN ISMAËL ●
The three-storey building, with its yellow gabled facade, houses exhibitions and event rooms as well as artists' studios. On display are contemporary artworks by Canary Island artists. *Tue–Sat 10am–1.30pm and 5pm–9pm | C. Almirante Lallermand 30*

INSIDER TIP ▶ PARQUE ESCULTÓRICO ●
Some of the island's other open spaces have in recent years also been embellished with sculptures and statues, but nowhere else are they as many or as interesting than in the island's capital. Apart from the almost 100 permanent sculptures (some with explanatory plaques) there are also the results of the sculptor symposium that has been held here since 2001. Most of the works adorn the promenade as well the extension on the rocky shore north of the large pier. But these are regularly replaced with the new exhibitions. A free route map is distributed by the tourist information centre and guides you through 16 of the town centre's art works. *www.turismo-puertodelrosario.org*

FOOD & DRINK

The same applies to all the venues in Puerto del Rosario: almost all of the staff only understand Spanish! If you would like something small to eat, there are three establishments that you can try: the ice-cream parlour *Kiss (C. Primero del Mayo, corner C. Maestro de Falla)*, the restaurant with a terrace *Los Paragüitas (at the harbour across from the tourist info)* and the bar and restaurant *Candela* which serves excellent tapas.

INSIDER TIP ▶ CANDELA
Right on the street, a café by day and a bar by night (dancing on Saturdays) it has a covered inner courtyard with a romantic

restaurant – a successful combination which makes 'the candle' a favourite destination for locals and tourists at any time of the day. *Daily | C. Fernández Castañeyra 10 | tel. 9 28 85 21 19 | Moderate–Expensive*

INSIDER TIP **LA TERRAZA DEL MUELLE ●** ☼

A table with a sea view is what you can expect at 'the terrace', in Puerto Rosario's chill out zone on the small beach. Trendy

The poet's desk in the Casa Museo Unamuno

EL CONGREJO COLORAO ☼

'The colourful crab' is a good choice for an affordable seafood meal with sea views. The best place is on the covered terrace right on the sea shore. Especially recommended is their three-course set menu. *Closed Sun evenings | C. Juan Ramón Jiménez 2 | from the harbour head north along the Calle Almirante Lallermand, after the petrol station take the next road right, motorists have to drive one street further then turn right and drive back | tel. 9 28 85 84 77 | Moderate*

SITIO

This is the town's leading gourmet restaurant. Trendy atmosphere and some unusual dishes like ostrich or kangaroo. *Closed Sun | C. La Cruz 26 | tel. 9 28 53 20 12 | Expensive*

but substantial meals with decent portions. *Closed Tue | Los Pozos, corner Guadiana | tel. 9 28 86 16 35 | Moderate–Expensive*

SHOPPING

☺ LA BIOSFERA

The weekly market on the top floor of the bus station was established especially to sell the island's produce – everything is very fresh and organic. *Estación de Guaguas | Sat 9am–2pm*

LAS ROTONDAS ●

Between the first and the second roundabout southwards is the town's very conspicuous shopping centre – a destination in itself. Almost 100 stores are spread over four floors and there is also a large parking garage. Instead of escalators, pram-friendly rolling ramps link the floors. In addition to the usual (clothing, sporting goods) you will also find telephone shops, a bookstore and a Hiperdino supermarket.

ENTERTAINMENT

If you are feeling adventurous and can speak a bit of Spanish, you should leave your resort for one INSIDER TIP Saturday night and explore the local nightlife. Nowhere on the island will you find such attractive and authentic bars and as much Latin dance fun as here (e.g. in the Mama Rumba). Bars and clubs only open at about 11pm and smart casual clothing is preferred, that means no sandals, running shoes, baseball caps or tee-shirts. In addition Puerto Rosario also offers some more sophisticated culture, like performances and art exhibitions in the *Casa de la Cultura (C. Ramiro de Maeztu 2)*. Events are advertised on posters in Spanish around the town.

CALLE 54
The nicest bar in town – quite large, with an inner courtyard, an authentic atmosphere and some modern art to admire. One of the best places to spend a Saturday night. *Northern end of the C. Secundino Alonso across from the sports hall.*

CAMELOT
This large nightclub takes up two floors and has been popular for years. It has TV screens for video clips and the music played includes hip hop, house and R&B. Occasionally also live music. *Thu–Sat from 11pm | C. León y Castillo 12 | entrance C. Ayose 6*

INSIDER TIP MAMA RUMBA
The most beautiful Latin American dance venue on the island has a wonderful relaxed atmosphere where every guest (regardless of age and ability) is made to feel welcome. Another excellent choice for Saturday nights. *C. San Roque 17 | close to Cabildo Insular*

Boats bobbing in the harbour at Puerto del Rosario

Puerto del Rosario

250 m
273 yd

Accommodation in Puerto del Rosario is very limited when it comes to tourists, because in the town itself there is no accommodation with terraces, entertainment and the usual tourist amenities.

HOTEL FUERTEVENTURA PLAYA BLANCA

This was once a *Parador Nacional* and has been redesigned to resemble a North African caravanserai – with swimming pool and beach access. The three star hotel with 50 rooms has an excellent restaurant, which is also worth a visit. *Tel. 9 28 85 11 50* | *Moderate–Expensive*

JM PUERTO ROSARIO

More of a business hotel but the only comfortable hotel that is centrally situated and almost all of the 88 rooms have a view of the harbour or sea. *Avda. Marítima 9* | *tel. 9 28 85 94 64* | *www.jmhoteles.com* | *Moderate*

ROQUEMAR

At the large roundabout below the León y Castillo is this 16 room hotel with a view of the harbour. It is not a very quiet place however, if you follow the insider tip about Saturday night (see p. 50) you can still have a good rest, because there is hardly any traffic on a Sunday morning. *Avda. Marítima 1 | tel. 9 28 53 36 46 | hotelroquemar@hotmail.com | Budget*

INFORMATION

PATRONATO DE TURISMO
Avda. Marítima at the large roundabout across C. León y Castillo | tel. 9 28 53 08 44

WHERE TO GO

CASILLAS DEL ÁNGEL
(126 C1) *(ﾉﾉ F6)*
In the small village between Puerto del Rosario and Betancuria, the white *Santa Ana Church* (dating back to the late 18th century) is worth a visit. The baroque front entrance is made from black lava rock. It is crowned by an open gable that serves as a bell tower and it has an ornamental altar that is very important to the island. An oil painting depicts the Last Judgement and you should also take a look at the beautiful ceiling panelled in the Mudéjar style *(key for the church obtainable from house no. 20 A, opposite the church entrance).*

TEFÍA
(126 C1) *(ﾉﾉ E6)*
From Casillas del Ángel (towards La Oliva) it is not far to Tefía – a scattered, rural settlement that is surrounded by mountains. Some of the older farmhouses

BOOKS & FILMS

▶ **Notes From the Canary Islands** – a very personal book by Camille Lenning that describes her travels through the islands, the eccentric and interesting locals she meets along the way, their customs and her adventures. Told in an intimate and conversational manner, it paints an entertaining and humorous account of the islands and their residents.

▶ **Pleasures of the Canary Islands: Wine, Food and Mystery** – this little book by husband and wife team Ann and Larry Walkers (he is a wine writer and she is a chef) takes the reader by the hand and sets off to explore the pleasures of the islands, the food, the wines, the nature and the people. It also includes a chapter with some traditional recipes.

▶ **Fuerteventura: Car Tours and Walks** – by Noel Rochford is a very handy guide to all the walking and driving routes on the island. There are detailed walks to suit all interests and fitness levels, from seaside hikes to mountain climbs and much more. Full of interesting background information as well as very practical information – like where to find petrol stations!

▶ **Clash of the Titans** (2010) and its sequel **Wrath of the Titans** (2012) – starring Liam Neeson and Ralph Fiennes were both filmed in parts on the Canary Islands and Fuerteventura. The fantasy film is plot is based on a Greek myth and Fuerteventura's clear skies, ample sun, beautiful scenery and dramatic landscapes made it an ideal location.

have been restored and included in the ★ ● *outdoor museum La Alcogida*. The houses have been restored by traditional craftsmen and there are even animals kept here. Find out more in the chapter 'Travel with kids'.

TETIR
(122–123 C–D6) (*M F5–6*)

From Puerto del Rosario you drive on the old main road to Corralejo, past the island's old airport *Los Estancos*. The old

prickly pears – are relics of an era when agriculture was still very important and provided the inhabitants with a degree of prosperity. Tetir's parish church (1745) the *Iglesia de Santo Domingo de Guzmán* with its baroque altar bears witness to this former prosperity. The characteristic white tower with the dark edges was only added 40 years later. In the square in front of the church, a statue commemorates the founder of the Banco de Canarias, a native of the village.

Goats in the outdoor museum La Alcogida in Tefir

landing strip crossed over the road which had to be closed every time an aeroplane took off or landed. On the left hand side are two abandoned airport terminals. The church village of *Tetir*, which was at one point the parish church of Puerto del Rosario, is the focal point of this fertile valley. The terraced fields on the valley slopes – once used to grow cereals and

It is worth making a detour to the 511m/ 1680ft high mountain ☆ INSIDER TIP *Temejereque* (123 D5) (*M F5*) north of Tetir. From the broadcasting station on the summit you have excellent views of the island on a clear day. The access road turns off about 1.5km/1mi north-west of Tetir. Straight ahead after the 'Tamariche' signpost.

THE CENTRE

It is also where you will have your first encounter with Fuerteventura, because it is here – south of the capital Puerto del Rosario – that you will land at the airport. The first impression is a sobering one: as you will see little more than the rather dull semi-industrial and commercial section of the town.

Tourists also seem to head straight out, either towards the north of the island or south to the Jandía peninsula. But at some point most tourists return to the centre region, because four of the islands five places of historic importance lie here: Antiqua, Betancuria, Pájara and Tuineje.

These towns all have some interesting museums focusing on religious, archaeological and agricultural history. The island's busiest tourist centre of Caleta de Fustes is also close to the airport while the bays of the south coast are lined with picturesque fishing villages. And friendly Gran Tarajal, the island's second largest city, is also here.

The area is divided into a wide, trough-shaped extended valley with a mountainous area to the west, which rises up to 722m/2370ft, and has deep valleys and beautiful palm oases. Some farming is still done here and the main produce are tomatoes and aloe vera.

Photo: Vega de Río de las Palmas

Quiet fishing villages and palm oases, high mountains and deep valleys: this is the historic centre of the island

ANTIGUA

(125 E3) (_m_ _E7–8_) Arriving from the north, you are welcomed to La Antigua by the windmill at the Molino de Antigua exhibition centre.

The town is surrounded by a wide valley that has been settled since the end of the 15th century when Andalusian and Norman settlers arrived and began to cultivate the red fertile valley soil. They also later founded La Antigua in the 18th century. During the 19th century the parish town was even the seat of the island's council for two years.

Today La Antigua also administers the surrounding community (with the same name) which also profits from tourism along with the holiday resort of Caleta de

ANTIGUA

Molina de Antigua: a beautifully restored gem set in a manicured garden

Fustes – part of the revenues are channelled into the large sport centre (with a wrestling arena for the traditional *lucha canaria*) south-east of the town.

SIGHTSEEING

CHURCH
The white parish church – dedicated to the Virgin of Antigua – dominates the centre of the community. The large building has a single nave and bell tower and was completed in 1785. Don't miss the Mudéjar ceiling in the choir and the ochre-coloured classical altar. In the courtyard plants bloom in almost sub-tropical opulence. *Daily 9am–1pm*

MOLINO DE ANTIGUA
The 'windmill of Antigua' is an eye-catching landmark in the village and is also the namesake of the facility (completed in 1998) that includes exhibition rooms, a well-stocked craft shop, a gallery, a beautiful cactus garden, a cafeteria and an archaeological collection from the lava tunnel of Villaverde. The inside of the mill can also be viewed. *On the FV 20 north of the town | Tue–Sat 10am–6pm | entrance 2 euro (shops and workshops often closed)*

WHERE TO STAY

INSIDER TIP ▶ **LA ERA DE LA CORTE** ●
The hotel with its lovely and authentic atmosphere was a pioneer in the island's rural tourism. There are only eleven rooms in this converted manor and it is ideal for guests looking for tranquillity and those who can do without the beach hustle and bustle. Its isolated location means that it is only an option for those with a rental car. A tennis court, small swimming pool and beautiful inner courtyard. *C. La Corte 1 | south of the town | tel. 9 28 87 87 05 | Moderate*

Information pavilion on the church square | daily 10am–2pm

WHERE TO GO

SAVIMAX ALOE VERA PLANTATION
(125 E3) *(ω E8)*

Here you can see this age-old medicinal plant up close, also on sale at the factory are the products that are derived from it. *At the roundabout on the FV 50 go 5km/ 3mi in the direction of Valles de Ortega, signposted*

POZO NEGRO AND THE ANCIENT SETTLEMENT RUINS AT ATALAYITA ●

Turn off the FV 2 on to the cul-de-sac road to Pozo Negro, after about 3km/1.8mi you will see a road that turns right on to a new track. It runs diagonally across the black lava flow that follows the road to the coast and leads to the most important ruins of structures built by the island's original inhabitants, pre-Spanish times (127 D5) *(ω F9)*. Excavations left of the road have uncovered various small igloo-like buildings made from lava rocks, many of which have been restored. It seems to have been a shepherd settlement and the shelters were not used as homes but rather as storage rooms and meat drying rooms. From the 15th century the basic rectangular ground floor plans were added to make the building larger, including some shelters for live stock. A small museum opposite the entrance provides information about the excavations. The solidified lava flow (the Malpaís Grande) where the goats of the indigenous Canary Island inhabitants roamed, was created by one of the island's last eruptions about ten thousand years ago. On the summit of the eastern hill, you can look out over the whole terrain.

The fishing village, Pozo Negro (black fountain) (127 D5) *(ω G9)* consists of little more than two rows of houses on a bay with a black pebble and dark sand beach. There are two lovely restaurants with sea views that serve fresh fish *(Budget)*.

TRIQUIVIJATE
(126 C2–3) *(ω F7)*

This little hamlet east of Antigua would not be worth the visit if it was not for the fine restaurant *El Jardín* where the Dutch proprietor and her Spanish husband serve excellent Spanish and international cuisine. From the 🌿 terrace you can look out over the landscape. *Mon–Wed and Sun evenings closed | coming from Antigua left at the roundabout, opposite Jordan (bar and shop)in the side street, then third house on the left | tel. 6 80 88 72 26 | Moderate–Expensive*

MARCO POLO HIGHLIGHTS

⭐ **Betancuria**
Church, cloister, and crafts – Fuerteventura's history lives on in this old mountain village
→ p. 58

⭐ **Barranco de las Peñitas**
Hike along the dam and down an isolated and rocky gorge
→ p. 60

⭐ **Pájara's parish church**
Village church with the famous Mexican baroque portal
→ p. 66

⭐ **Oasis Park**
Take time out from the beach and spend an interesting day at the cactus garden and zoo
→ p. 69

BETANCURIA

(125 D3) (*∅ D7*) ★ ● **This is the most historic town on the island. It was founded in 1405 by the Norman Jean de Béthencourt, who conquered the island in the name of the Castilian crown.**

Here, in a fertile valley, protected by high mountains, he found the ideal site for a residence. He soon left to travel further and although no bishop has ever lived here, the town has the status of a bishopric. The little village (600 inhabitants) can only be reached via a winding mountain road. It is very pretty with a number of restored old mansions. Life here is heavily influenced by tourism. *Park at the southern entrance, then walk to the church*.

SIGHTSEEING

CASA SANTA MARÍA

The most beautiful features of the island are shown here, and not just in the main attraction, the amazing ● INSIDER TIP multi-media show (last show 3.30pm). The historical photos and farming equipment as well as an embroidery demonstration are also very interesting; linger in the peaceful shaded garden. *Entrance past the restaurant with the same name | Mon–Sat 10am–4pm | entrance 5 euro*

CONVENTO DE SAN BUENAVENTURA

In the valley before the northern entrance of the town are the ruins of a 17th century Franciscan monastery. Since the secularization of the monastery in 1836, the citizens have used the site as a stone quarry which is why the cloister is gone. Opposite the church is a chapel. It was built in front of a cave where, during the 15th century, San Diego (a miracle worker and missionary) was believed to have lived.

CHURCH

The current *Iglesia de Santa María* that towers over the valley floor was built in 1620 as a replacement to the first cathedral. The first cathedral was built in 1593, shortly after the town was founded, but it was destroyed by pirates. The triple-naved church is built in the island's typical Mudéjar style (with wooden ceilings) and contains a number of altars. Amongst them a beautiful baroque main altar that dates back to 1684. In the right niche of the left altar on the northern wall (opposite the entrance) is a wood carved statue of Santa Catalina. It is regarded as one of the oldest surviving works of art on the island. The sacristy with its carved and painted wooden ceiling is another attraction *(entrance left of the altar room). Mon–Sat 11am–4pm | entrance 1.50 euro (including Museo de Arte Sacro)*

MUSEO ARQUEOLÓGICO

The museum is on the main road and is guarded by two canons that were captured from English pirates in 1740 during the Battle of Tamacite. Displays of photos and texts tell the history of the indigenous population and their culture. *Mon–Sat 10am–6pm | entrance 2 euro | on the main road*

MUSEO DE ARTE SACRO

In the rectory close to the church is a small – but priceless – collection of religious art and artefacts. *Currently closed due to construction; ask the church supervisor*

FOOD & DRINK

For a snack, go to *Princess Arminda* with its patio (above the church square) or the *Casa Santa María cafeteria*, which serves drinks and homemade cake in a separate part of the garden *(entrance is behind the church | both Budget)*.

INSIDER TIP **CASA SANTA MARÍA**

The *Casa Santa María*, an award-winning restaurant that is stylish without being over-the-top. The two inner courtyards are both a sheer delight. The kitchen serves sophisticated traditional dishes. *Daily Sun 11.30am–5.30pm | at the church square | tel. 928 87 82 82 | Expensive*

SHOPPING

In various shops close to the church – especially in the *Casa Santa María* – you will find the best and most varied range of arts and crafts on sale. The items are from all over the island and include prickly pear jam and jars of ready-made mojo sauce.

WHERE TO GO

TEGÚ ☸ **(125 D3)** *(𝄞 D7)*

From the top of the pass north of the town (there is also a place to stop along the road) you will get a lovely view of the island's old capital, and of the northern part of the island all the way up to the shifting sand dunes of Corralejo. The viewing point and car park is dominated by two large statues, which represent the ancient Fuerteventura kings (or chiefs) Guise and Ayose – heroic images of rather dubious artistic value. The well designed viewing point ● *Mirador Morro Velosa* higher up at 640m/2100ft also offers impressive panoramic views of the landscape *(with conference venue and café | Tue–Sat 10am–6pm)*.

VEGA DE RÍO DE LAS PALMAS,
THE DAM AND BARRANCO DE
LAS PEÑITAS (124 C 3–4) *(𝄞 C–D8)*

About 6km/3.7mi south of Betancuria is one of the island's most beautiful palm tree oases. The farming settlement was briefly called Vega de Río Palma. Today only potatoes and a few vegetables are

Six hundred years of history: Betancuria

cultivated on the small fields. The 17th century village church on the left hand side *(daily 10.30am–1pm, 4pm–6.30pm)* has the largest shrine on the island: a 23cm/9inch alabaster figurine of the Virgen de la Peña, Virgin Mary with Child. This figure of Mary is thought to be the oldest on the island and was brought here towards Pájara, as the main road starts to climb, take a right turn into the valley at Vega de Río Palma (signposted) and go a further 1300m where the road crosses the creek for a second time and park your car. From there you can walk down the valley along the dry river bed towards the dam. After 15 minutes, just before the

The goal of every hike through the Barranco de las Peñitas is the Ermita de la Peña

from France during the 15th century by the conqueror Jean de Béthencourt. As patron saint of the island the shrine is the destination of the largest pilgrimage on the island. At the church square, the lovely courtyard restaurant *Don Antonio,* is a great place to recharge. *(Tue–Sun 11am–5pm | tel. 9 28 87 87 57 | Expensive).* At the southern end of the oasis you can go on one of the most beautiful hikes that the island has to offer in the rocky ★ *Barranco de las Peñitas* gorge. Drive tamarisk forest, leave the river bed to the right (just after another distinctive path that also turns right) and continue above the forest and then along the *Embalse de las Peñitas* dam and after about 10–15 minutes you will reach the dam wall. Just beyond the dam wall the path splits in two and leads down to the dramatic rocky gorge of the Barranco de las Peñitas. After a few minutes you will reach the white-washed *Ermita de la Peña* chapel, a cool, peaceful place of rest. When the wind blows through the rocks here it makes some rather eerie sounds, like the whispers of a ghostly choir! To return you backtrack on the same path. The whole hike should take about 90 minutes (including a bit of a break). At some places you will need to be very sure-footed and don't forget to take some water!

GOAT FARM (125 D3) (*D7*)

From the Finca de Pepe car park go through the barn to the cheese factory, where you can see how the cheeses are produced and where you can also buy a selection of goat's cheese and other goat's milk products. *From the FV 30 opposite the monastery ruins 1.6km/1mi downhill*

CALETA DE FUSTES

(127 E3) (*G8*) **This holiday resort was developed in the 1980s and lies on a gently curved south facing bay on the island's east coast, just 7km/4.5mi from the airport.**

It is very popular with British holidaymakers. In brochures, maps and signs it is also referred to as Costa Caleta, Playa de Castillo, Castillo de Fuste or El Castillo. The *'castillo'* refers to the *Castillo de Fustes*, a round, stone tower that was built in 1740 as the town's defence against pirates. Today it forms part of the bungalow hotel complex, *El Castillo*. There is no historic town centre, but the few modern shopping centres have some restaurants and bars and are a good substitute. The island's capital is also nearby (hourly bus service). Despite the fact that the area surrounding Caleta de Fustes is not very attractive, the town is growing rapidly: in the south around the golf course and then also stretching out along the coast with large hotels, like the CC Atlántico, now obstructing the view of the sea.

FOOD & DRINK

There is a vibrant selection of international restaurants in the *El Castillo* shopping centre near the beach, *the Castillo Centro* a little further on and in the *Happy Center*. The best spot for an outdoor snack is at *El Camarote* and the neighbouring café, *Panycreps* in the harbour or at the very pleasant INSIDER TIP beach bar *La Isla* which is on a man-made island in the south of the bay and can only be reached via a bridge, they also serve meals *(Moderate)*. The best cheesecake on offer is at *Café Mozart (CC Atlántico, street level, sea facing)*.

LA PAELLA

This is without a doubt the best dining option. There is no better place to enjoy a delicious meal than at one of their white-clothed tables on the sheltered terrace overlooking the bay, watching the sun as it sets. Mediterranean cuisine. *Daily | Barceló Castillo Beach Resort | eastern end of the bay, entrance from the promenade | tel. 928163100 (ext. 527) | Moderate*

TAPAS

The most authentically Spanish venue in town, it only attracts a few tourists making it ideal for connoisseurs. The tapas are not cheap but you can share, and they also have an affordable lunch menu. *C. Alcalde Francisco B. Jordan close to the country road | tel. 928163199 | Moderate*

SHOPPING

The shopping centres all carry a large, international selection of products. Saturday is market day: carvings, clothes, jewellery and much more *(9am–2pm | in the west near to the country road).* The most popular supermarket is the *Padilla* in the *CC Atlántico.*

SPORTS & ACTIVITIES

The protected bay is ideal for beginner windsurfers and *Fuerte Fun Center* offers courses *(at the western end of the beach | www.fuerte-surf.com).* The colourful marine life at the *Oceanarium* in the harbour is a pleasure for both young and old but there are also many other options: peddle boats or jet-skiing, deep sea fishing, underwater submarine (or semi-submarine) trips as well as dolphin and whale watching trips. There are also viewing pontoons so you can see fish up close: when you feed them they come up to the surface. The latest attraction is to go swimming with seals *(tel. 9 28 16 35 14).* Also at the harbour: the diving school *Deep Blue (tel. 9 28 16 37 12 | www.deep-blue-diving. com).*

At the hotel *Geranios (tel. 2 72 20 01 90), Caleta Cycles* hires out bicycles, while motorcycles and scooters can be hired from *East Coast Rides (CC Castillo Center | tel. 6 93 24 92 45 | www.fuerteventurarides. com).* INSIDER TIP ▶ Cool Runnings has the best offer for couples: the choice of chauffeur driven rides or driving yourself *(Hotel Elba San Jorge | tel. 9 28 54 75 13 | www. fuertetrikes.com).*

The shallow beach is great for children and those learning to swim. For spa and wellness treatments the best option is the ● thalassotherapy centre at the hotel *Barceló Fuerteventura.* It is part of the hotel but is open to the public and their treatments include: beauty treatments, chocolate therapy, wine massages, Ayurveda and shiatsu, seaweed baths and many more.

South of the town there are two 18-hole golf courses next to each other: the *Fuerteventura Golf Club (tel. 9 28 16 00 34 | www.fuerteventuragolfclub.com)* and the *Golf Club Salinas de Antigua (tel. 9 28 87 72 72 | www.salinasgolf.com).* The former is also the oldest and largest of the two with long stretches, but both are par 70 and have views of the Atlantic.

ENTERTAINMENT

Holidaymakers, particularly in CC El Castillo, are usually in high spirits so there is usually a party atmosphere in places like *Piero's.* There are sea views and good cocktails at the *Beach Café (until 10pm | western end of the beach, Hotel Geranios).*

WHERE TO STAY

BARCELÓ CASTILLO BEACH RESORT
This large complex consists of 390 apartments and bungalows – all with their own balcony or terrace – and is situated directly on the beach. It has a large seawater swimming pool area grouped around the old defence tower. Also freshwater pools (heated in winter), a plaza with restaurants, shops, bars, cafés, a yacht marina, tennis courts and entertainment. *Tel. 9 28 16 31 01 | www.barcelo.com | Moderate*

BARCELÓ FUERTEVENTURA
All your needs will be catered to here: Caribbean flair, sea views from all the 462 rooms, direct beach access, huge pools (one heated), mini golf, tennis, saunas, entertainment for young and old and many other pleasures. *Tel. 9 28 54 75 17 | www.barcelo.com | Moderate*

ELBA PALACE GOLF
Only 61 rooms all in an elegant Canarian style. The hotel has direct access to the northern golf course. *At the western end of the Golf Club Fuerteventura | tel. 9 28 16 39 22 | www.hoteleselba.com | Expensive*

Why do we need salt? Displays in the Salinas des Carmen salt museum

INFORMATION

OFICINA DE TURISMO
West of CC Centro Castillo | tel. 9 28 16 32 86

WHERE TO GO

SALINAS DEL CARMEN AND PUERTO DE LA TORRE (127 E4) *(Ø G8–9)*
Almost 3km/2mi south of Caleta de Fustes you turn left to the *Salinas del Carmen* salt pans and the *Salt Museum*. The road leads directly up to the entrance and the visitor's centre which you should visit first before walking through the salt pans. For demonstration purposes the salt pans are still operated in the traditional manner. At the water's edge there is also a massive whale skeleton on show *(Tue–Sat 10am–6pm | entrance 5 euro)*. Down in the little village INSIDER TIP Los Caracolitos has made a name for itself as one of the best fish restaurants in the area *(closed Wed | tel. 9 28 17 42 42 | Budget)*. Roughly 1500m further south are the steep ravines of the palm studded *Barranco de la Torre* valley with the ruins of an old lime kiln and the old harbour *Puerto de la Torre* at its estuary.

LAS PLAYITAS

(131 E4–5) *(Ø E11)* **The name 'the little beaches' refers to the peaceful fishing village at the end of the road.**
The larger of the small beaches is separated from the village by a hill and has been developed into a holiday destination for families and sports enthusiasts. In the picturesque old village, with its whitewashed houses, visitors and locals alike are attracted by the modest promenade

and the small pier where fishermen still land their catches.

FOOD & DRINK

In the village *La Rampa de Tío Enrique* serves traditional dishes as well as freshly caught fish – with a sea view *(closed Tue | at the pier | Moderate)*. The *Playitas Grand Resort* offers two à-la-carte restaurants, both have terraces and sea views: *La Bodega* with Spanish cuisine *(only Wed– Sun evenings| Moderate)* and the Italian *Trattorio Da Luigi (Budget–Moderate)*. They are both situated on the Plaza Rambla close to the resort hotel *Cala del Sol*.

SPORTS & ACTIVITIES

The *Grand Resort* is a sports resort geared towards both amateurs and professionals and it has the only Olympic sized swim-ming pool on the island. Other facilities include tennis courts, a large fitness cen-tre, the *Cycle Center* with bicycle hire and organised bicycle tours, a scuba diving school *Deep Blue (tel. 6 53 51 26 38 | www. deep-blue-diving.com)* and a surf and sail-ing school *Cat Company (tel. 6 16 61 93 13 | http://catcompany.eu)*. The showpiece of the *Playitas Grand Resort* is its 18 hole golf course. It is open to the public and not just for hotel guests however, hotel guests do get a discount. They also offer golf les-sons for beginners and advanced players (complete courses or hourly) and have a driving range and a putting green (book-ings at *www.playitas.info*).

WHERE TO STAY

PLAYITAS GRAND RESORT
Everything is close together here: a fam-ily and child-friendly hotel on the eastern

There is seldom a crowd on the harbour promenade at Las Playitas seaside and the elegant hotel *Cala del Sol* as well as the bungalow complex *Villas Playitas*. All three of them surround the golf course and all hotels have direct beach access. *Tel. 928 86 04 00 | www. playitas.info | Moderate–Expensive*

WHERE TO GO

INSIDER TIP **GRAN TARAJAL**
(131 D5) (*Ø E11*)

This sleepy little port town (10,000 citizens, 5km/3mi west of Las Playitas) whose name means 'big tamarisk' does not have anything special about it. But, if you have been here once, you might be amongst those who keep returning. Before you enter the town you pass a palm grove, park your car in the centre, linger around for a moment and listen to the murmur of the fountain on the shady main square and then walk a little further to the ● broad beach promenade. After your stroll you should take a seat in one of the local restaurants. You can look out over the black sandy beach to the glittering sea and watch the activity on the beach feeling wonderfully at ease …

For a bite to eat – with a panoramic view of the beach – try *Panna & Pomodoro*, the best place on the promenade: cheap and good *(Budget)*. The 🕒 Gran Tarajal beach is a green flag beach. Green flags are awarded for sustainability, i.e. using environmental standards in the management of the beach.

At the 39.7km/25mi point on the road to Tuineje – north of the major road junction on the right hand side – you can sample goat's cheese in its four different stages of maturity at the *Quesería Maxorata* dairy.

PUNTA DE LA ENTALLADA
(131 E4) (*Ø F11*)

At Las Playitas an asphalt road turns off to the east. It leads (6km/3.7mi) to the

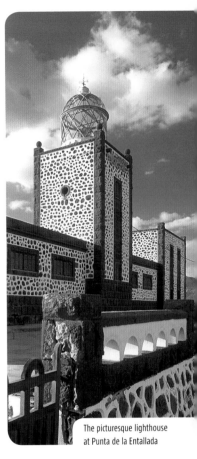

The picturesque lighthouse at Punta de la Entallada

south-eastern cape *Punta de la Entallada* which has a picturesque ⚓ lighthouse on its highest point.

PÁJARA

(124 C4) (*Ø C–D9*) **This well-kept hamlet lies in a deep valley and is surrounded by 600m/1968ft mountains that protect it from the harsh winds and make it green, lush and shady.**

The entire south-west of the island is administered by Pájara and one can sense the prosperity that tourism has brought to the region, for example, in the modern town hall and in the fact that the town has the only public swimming pool on the island.

The small terraced fields on the surrounding slopes bear witness to the fact that this area was also once intensively cultivated. The valley soil was very fertile and the community (dominated by a few land owners) worked and cultivated the land, ensuring prosperity for their secular and ecclesiastical lords. The largest legacy from that period is the parish church. *Parking space in the barranco below the church and town hall | access from the road from Betancuria*

SIGHTSEEING

PARISH CHURCH ★

The nave of the *Iglesia Nuestra Señora de Regla* was built during the 17th century to the beginning of the 18th century. The church became known for its beautiful Mexican baroque façade with Aztec elements. In addition to the geometric sun patterns it also has snakes, panthers and birds. It was, for a long time, a mystery as to how the stone portal could have been transported all the way from Mexico to this remote place. Today however, we know that an unknown stonemason must have copied the patterns from an Italian sample book and that neither the stone nor the portal façade came from Mexico. The dark interior of the church has two naves decorated with a wooden ceiling in the Mudéjar style. The Mudéjar style developed during the 14th/15th century in Spain as a combination of the Moorish and Gothic style and was used for a long time on the island. The beautifully gilded baroque altar was completed in 1785. In the afternoons when the sun shines it seems as if the altar is lit up by spotlights – thanks to small windows that were built so high up that you cannot see them from the church's interior. Right at the entrance is a machine that lights up the alter for a euro. *Daily 10am–2.30pm, Sun until 4.30pm*

FOOD & DRINK

INSIDER TIP ▶ CASA ISAÍTAS

Careful restoration work transformed this 200-year-old ruin into a real gem: an intimate four-roomed guesthouse (*Expensive*) with two beautiful inner courtyards and an atmospheric, good restaurant that is famous for its choice of delicious tapas. *Closed Mon–Thu evenings, in August also closed Thu | opposite the parking lot below the church | tel. 928 16 14 02 | www.casaisaitas.com | Moderate*

WHERE TO GO

AJUY/PUERTO DE LA PEÑA
(124 B3) (∅ C8)

This fishing village (with two names) is a popular sightseeing destination. Electricity and running water were only introduced in 1986. Those in need of some sustenance should go to the 'golden cage' the *Jaula*

Puerto de la Peña is also the starting point of two short hikes. On the north end of the beach the hike leads like a ramp over a rocky plateau to the *Caleta Negra* bay where enormous caves have been eroded by the action of the sea. Walk across the plateau to the north, past the old lime kilns (two small gorges below) and follow the path along the water to the steep downhill steps. A high concrete pillar that was part of the old dock is visible. At the foot of the pillar you will be at the entrance to the larger of the two 'pirate caves'. The second cave is just next to it.

Hiking trail with a sea view at Ajuy/Puerto de la Peña

de Oro (Moderate). Its prime location, directly on the beach, is reflected in its prices and service. A more affordable alternative is *Casa Pepin (Budget)* higher up on the slope but still with a lovely sea view from the terrace.

A second destination is the impressive INSIDER TIP rock arch that rises at the mouth of the *Barranco de la Peña* north of Ajuy. You reach it by following the road that branches off at the highest point that leads to the cave, continue above the

Caleta Negra, then go inland up to the next path running north to the *barranco* then turn left. In front of the rock arch is a natural swimming pool, perfect to cool off in.

TARAJALEJO

(130 B5) *(㎝ C12)* **On a long black sand and pebble beach on the southern coast is a small fishing village with a simple holiday complex nestled next to it.**
In recent years a hotel complex right on the beach, the *Bahía Playa with a variety of sporting activities, has also been added.*

FOOD & DRINK

LA BARRACA
Dine on a terrace that is right on the beach. Very simple and also very affordable. Good coffee. *Closed Sun | C. Isidro Díaz | tel. 9 28 16 10 89 | Budget*

SPORTS & ACTIVITIES

The *Windsurfcenter* on the beach side of the hotel offers the new sport of stand up paddling as well as catamaran sailing, kayaking, surfing and snorkelling and bicycle hire *(tel. 9 28 16 13 99 | http://water sports-fuerteventura.com)* while *CRC Bikes* hires out motorcycles and also arranges quad tours. *C. La Marisma | tel. 9 28 16 13 72*

WHERE TO STAY

BAHÍA PLAYA
The only holiday hotel in the village was built in 2007 and it is ideally situated right on the beach. Of the 172 rooms, 95 are spacious junior suites. Three swimming

No petting: the crocodile pool at the Oasis Park in La Lajita

pools and entertainment. *Tel. 9 28 16 10 01 | www.r2hotels.com | Moderate*

WHERE TO GO

OASIS PARK ⭐
(129 B5) (*M C12*)

What started out as a sad, beach zoo in the 1990s has evolved into one of the main attractions on the island. Here you can enjoy yourself all day long, and if you come back a year later you will be amazed what has been added as the park is constantly expanding and reinventing itself. The nucleus of the zoo is a spacious shady park with tall trees and flowering shrubs and the highlight of the visit is the very funny INSIDER TIP► parrot show and three open-air theatres, one each for reptiles, birds of prey and brilliantly trained seals. An open bus travels around the 40 acres of cactus garden which has over 2000 plant species and the birds of prey theatre. On offer are several outdoor cafés, a nursery, a well-stocked home and garden shop and the popular camel safaris! *For times and prices see 'Travel with kids' | on the FV 2 at La Lajita*

TUINEJE

(125 D5) (*M D–E9*) **This village is the Cinderella amongst the old island communities. Its main produce is the tomatoes that are grown under protective sun shades. They are also sorted and packed here. The tomatoes are protected from the wind and sun thus reducing the amount of water needed to irrigate them.**

For the islanders, Tuineje is forever associated with the memory of a glorious event in their history. In 1740 a group of English privateers landed in what is today called Gran Tarajal, and plundered and looted their way up to Tuineje where 37 intrepid farmers (under the leadership of the island commanders) succeeded in slaying almost half of the well-armed invaders which far outnumbered them. They managed this feat with the help of three dozen camels – which they used as shields – and only five guns and a hastily thrown together plan. The rest of the privateers fled. Apart from capturing several muskets during the siege/fight, the islanders also managed to secure two cannons which now decorate the entrance of the museum in Betancuria. This event is known as the Battle of Tamacite and the memory of the victory remains alive in two ways. First, the parish church *San Miguel* (late 18th century) which is surrounded by a defence wall, houses a visual display of the siege (two panels at the base of the altar) and secondly, the event is commemorated annually with a lavish historical fiesta at the end of September. The key to the church can be obtained in the house that has a rather striking commemorative plaque for a pious nun.

WHERE TO GO

MILL MUSEUM
(125 D4) (*M E9*)

About 204km/126mi north from Tuineje on the FV is Tiscamanita and its mill museum *(Centro de Interpretación de los Molinos)* which is housed in a restored windmill with adjoining farm buildings. It has a well-preserved collection that provides insights into Fuerteventura's tradition-rich milling trade and millrighting history. Every guest receives a complimentary sample of *gofio*. *Tue–Sat 10am–6pm | entrance 2 euro | coming from Tuineje behind Bar Tío Pepe turn left off the FV 20, then right*

THE SOUTH

This is the picture book part of Fuerteventura – nothing but sun, sand and sea. On the 20km/12mi stretch of Playas de Sotavento's beaches you can enjoy sea views from (almost) all the hotel room windows. Out on the waves the sails of the windsurfers add bright splashes of colour. Even at the largest holiday resorts – like the Costa Calma in the northeast and Morro Jable/Jandía Playa in the south – the beaches are never crowded and there is always plenty of space.

Everywhere along this coast the surf is gentle and although there is a constant wind, it is seldom unpleasant. On the Costa Calma and at the lagoons of Playa Barca the wind is generally stronger. Further south the mountains temper the breeze a little bit.

The area was first discovered as a tourist destination by a few Germans, who established the first holiday accommodation with the then *Casa Atlántica* and successfully brought the area's pristine beaches to the attention of two German tour operators. Shortly after that, in 1970, the first Robinson Club hotel was built on the former salt marshes. The Robinson Club name was very apt, because apart from tiny Morro Jable, the Jandía peninsula was almost entirely deserted back then. Even the hour long trip from the old

Bustle, bungalows and bathing fun on the one side and the isolated open spaces of the Jandía peninsula on the other

airport, Los Estancos west of Puerto del Rosario, was an adventure in itself when it seemed as if the gravel road wanted to rattle the bus – already an old vintage – apart bit by bit.

The Playas de Sotavento is only one side – actually just a half – of the coin, because the Jandía peninsula stretches beyond the southern cape at Morro Jable another 17km/10.5mi to the west, and on the other side is the long and elongated north-west coast. A trip in an off-road vehicle to these long, sandy and wonderfully isolated beaches is one of the highlights of a holiday on Fuerteventura. Between the two coasts is mountain country with *Pico de Jandía* its highest cloud covered peak at 807m/2647.6ft.

Even today most of Jandía remains deserted. Because of its ecological impor-

One of the Costa Calma's perfect beaches

tance the whole peninsula has been declared a natural park (with the exception of the inhabited coastal regions). Especially in the area of the Istmo de la Pared with its massive wind farm, tall fences have been put up to keep out the voracious goats and to give the vegetation a chance to grow.

COSTA CALMA

(129 F4) (ℳ B12) Costa Calma, or the 'calm coast', is the name that refers to the wide holiday zone on the Istmo de la Pared at the beginning of the Jandía peninsula.

This part that lies furthest east, is also known as Cañada del Río. The flat terrain on both sides of the main road has allowed – and still allows – building and over the years many bungalow and apartment complexes have sprung up. In between them are also some larger hotels but they are relatively unobtrusive (visually) and the rather unexpectedly lush green forest alongside the country road is what makes the biggest impression.

Costa Palma is spread out and there is no real village centre. Between the scattered holiday zones there are sections of fallow lands. Yet as a guest, you will not want for anything. After all what more do you need than the hot sun, a sandy beach and sparkling clear water? The sea front, that stretches out for miles, can sometimes be a bit crowded, yet the beaches stay pristine – obviously the guests also do their bit not to litter – and the water is, like everywhere on the island, of exceptional quality.

FOOD & DRINK

Restaurants are scattered around but the main focus is in the various shopping centres. *Fuerte Action (CC El Palmeral near the petrol station)* is popular from breakfast until late at night while the *Café Berlin* in the *CC Botánico* is famous for their delicious fresh pastries and cakes. Just one floor up is *Casa Nostra* where you will find the best Italian ice-cream in the area.

ARENA
Friendly and good, a little more expensive but better than *Mamma Mia* that is across the road. *Closes Sat. | CC Costa Calma | Budget–Moderate*

COPA
A restaurant run by expats, the owners Angelika and Paul have been serving up good quality food for many years. A welcoming atmosphere, the menu changes often, half portions are served on request and there are also English menus. *Only Fri–Tue evenings | at the parking lot above the CC El Palmeral (close to the petrol station | tel. 6 46 75 53 05 | Moderate*

INSIDER TIP EL DIVINO
'The divine or heavenly' – the name conjures up high expectations and you will not be disappointed! This also applies to the restaurant's beautiful interior and terrace, which is romantically lit with torches. The delicious dishes are a 'heavenly' fusion between traditional Canarian and European cuisine. And to top it all, the entire experience is amazingly affordable. *Only Wed–Mon evenings | C. Risco Blanco | tel. 6 19 10 33 42 | Moderate*

GALERIA
Another friendly expat restaurant which serves tapas and home-baked cakes. The terrace at the back has a view of the sea and can also be heated when necessary. *Tue–Sun from 6pm | C. Risco Blanco (third street south of CC Bahía Calma) | tel. 9 28 87 54 16 | Moderate*

INSIDER TIP EL PATIO
Dine beneath palm trees on the beach on a lovely wind-sheltered terrace (heated on cool evenings). There is very personal service and pleasant European-Canarian cuisine with fresh ingredients and good wine. *Mon–Sat, evenings only | in the Bungalow Hotel Solyventura, south of the beach at the tall palm trees | tel. 9 28 54 71 65 | www.solyventura.com | Moderate*

SHOPPING

There are about seven, mostly small shopping centres, spread through the holiday zone. The largest supermarket is in the new *CC Bahía Calma* while the shops in the *CC Sotavento (opposite the Hotel Taro Beach)* stock the largest range of wristwatches, jewellery, cosmetics and sunglasses. The *CC El Palmeral* close to the petrol station, is the most interesting with shops like Hodge Podge Fuerte with its sportswear, or the surf shop Fuerte Action,

★ Playa Barca
South of Costa Calma the wind, sand and waves have created a wonderfully endless beach → p. 79

★ Dunes at Risco del Paso
Sand dunes and secluded little hollows at the southern end of the lagoon → p. 81

★ Western cape and Cofete
An amazing vantage point, isolated beaches where you can experience the island's raw nature – and speculate about the mysterious Villa Winter → p. 89

MARCO POLO HIGHLIGHTS

and the great jewellery and mineral shop, Shop 1st One which is an attraction in itself. In the INSIDERTIP *Boutique Tangente* Bea Stein, who has been living on the island for years, sells original ready to wear clothing collections. Ask about her fashion shows *(in the hotel Costa Palma Palace, one floor below reception)*.

They also have a waterski school for beginners. However they are only open at certain times.

BICYCLE/MOTORBIKE

Volcano Bike will deliver a mountain bike to your hotel for you, they also offer guided tours *(tel. 6 39 73 87 43, Ralph)*. Off-road

Not for everyone: exciting but noisy jet ski fun on the water

The German bookstore in the *CC Costa Calma* also has a selection of English magazines, books and newspapers.
The market that travels around the island in weekly cycles comes to Coast Calma on Wednesdays and Sundays. Most of the goods on sale are African *(9am–2pm | at the large roundabout)*.

SPORTS & ACTIVITIES

JET SKI, WATERSKI

There is a jet ski and waterski base at the eastern edge of the bay where you can also hire banana boats and peddle boats.

dirt bike and quad tours (and off-road rentals) are offered by *Sahara Sports | tel. 6 06 60 00 90 Frank)*. Xtreme offers quad and buggy tours and also hire out bicycles *(at the Hotel Taro Beach | tel. 9 28 87 56 30)*. Whether with motor or muscle power: do not miss out on the INSIDERTIP guided tours.

SCUBA DIVING

Harry runs the scuba diving centre *Harry's Dive Base* in the Hotel Playa Esmeralda *(entrance next to the hotel | tel. 6 79 80 99 87)*, Simona and Kay run *Fuerte Divers* in the Hotel Costa Calma Beach *(second to last hotel before the northern edge of the beach | entrance through the hotel garden). Their diving school has two powerfully motorised dinghies and take divers out to some sunken wrecks off the coast (tel. 9 28 87 53 83 | www.fuerte divers.com). Other diving schools available in Sotavento Beach Club in the Morasol and in the Meliá Gorriones.

SURFING

For some real fast paced surfing you can be collected from the hotel in La Pared by one of the surf experts like *Waveguru* → p. 78. The best waves on the island can be found on the western coast of Fuerteventura.

WINDSURFING

Beginners and experts alike will find the best service at *Fuerte Fun Center (at the beach in front of the Monica Beach Club | tel. 9 28 87 53 83 www.fuerte-surf.com/ costa/en-index.html)*. At the world famous windsurfing beach of Playa Barca (129 E4) (*Ⓜ B12*) the *Pro Center René Egli* not only offer rentals and courses but also something for funboard specialists and kitesurfers – a real adventure! *At the hotel Meliá Gorriones | tel. 9 28 54 74 83 | www.rene-egli.com (with webcam)*

ENTERTAINMENT

ENTERTAINMENT

Not much happens late at night in Costa Calma, but there are few places (besides the hotels) that are interesting. Surfers meet at the *Green Room (Wed–Sat from 9pm | CC Internacional at the petrol station)* where there is usually a DJ so on weekends around midnight it usually gets quite full. The same goes for the INSIDER TIP bar and lounge *El Divino* next to the restaurant with the same name, where the great atmosphere and ambience appeals to a wide range of ages

(Wed–Sun from 10pm | C. Risco Blanco). For a cocktail without the noise a good option in the bar *Synergy (Mon–Sat from 7pm | CC Costa Calma)*. In the basement there is also a pub, the *Bodega Romántica (closed Mon)*. Next door in the disco the party really only starts after midnight.

WHERE TO STAY

BAHÍA CALMA

The bright white, cleverly designed 75 bungalows and 45 apartments are grouped around a pool and the beach, restaurant and two shopping centres are all close by. At night the rustle of the palm trees will send you off to sleep. *Tel. 9 28 54 71 58 | Moderate*

BUNGALOW HOTEL SOLYVENTURA

The 18 residential units of this exclusive resort all have large individual terraces and sea views – some even from the bed – as well as direct beach access. If you are not after fitness centres or discos, but prefer a personal atmosphere along with beautiful peaceful surroundings and great views, you will find it here. *C. Punta de Barlovento 22 | tel. 9 28 54 71 65 | www. solyventura.com | Expensive*

LOW BUDGET

▶ All the scuba diving schools offer free trial lessons and even though they take place in the hotel pool, they are enough to give you an idea of how it is done.

▶ Oh, là là – only two euro for a small breakfast! The *Café Oh là là* in Costa Calma serves a cheap and delicious breakfast. *CC Costa Calma*

COSTA CALMA

COSTA CALMA PALACE

This is truly a palace – a four star hotel that has nine storeys and a massive resort building that dominates the area. The guests – mostly adults wanting to get away from it all for some peace and quiet – enjoy sea views from all the 417 rooms, breakfast underneath the palm trees and a comprehensive wellness programme with salt water swimming pools and thallaso therapy. There are two tennis courts and a golf practice facility. *Avda. Jahn Reisen | tel. 9 28 87 60 10 | www.sbhoteles.es | Expensive*

MARYVENT

This is a complex of 54 self-catering apartments (in different sizes) that is located right on the beach and is spread over three storeys. Each has its own kitchen and balcony and most have sea views. *Below the shopping centre Bahía Calma II | tel. 9 28 54 73 92 | www.maryvent. com | Moderate*

PLAYA ESMERALDA

One of the features of this comfortable, 333 room hotel is the fact that it has direct access to the beach, it also has good cuisine, affordable prices and an indoor swimming pool for inclement days. *At the southern edge of the resort | tel. 9 28 87 53 53 | http://h10hotels.com | Moderate*

RISCO DEL GATO

This small but discerning bungalow hotel (51 units) was seen as an architectural sensation when it opened. Accommodation is in low private bungalows with shell-shaped roofs each with an intimate sun terrace that is protected from the north-east trade winds and from prying eyes. The complex has swimming pools, a sauna, tennis court, cafeteria and restaurant. *At the southern edge of the resort | tel. 9 28 54 71 75 | www.vikhotels.com | Expensive*

MELIÁ GORRIONES (129 D5) (*M A13*)

Its wonderful location, far from other hotels in a nature reserve and just above the lagoon of the Playa Barca, makes it quite special. After a total renovation, the 418 room hotel (they also have spacious family rooms), now has a new lease on

BAD INVESTMENTS

The enormous tourism revenues generated by some of the island's communities have been too tempting and there have been some morals corrupted along the way. While the mayor beguiled the citizens of La Oliva with a magnificent (and seldom used) public swimming pool and thus secured his re-election, Casa del Inglés the stately mansion in Corralejo falls further into ruin. Investments in tourism have also not always been successful. Excellent examples of this are the building excavations and unfinished streets north of El Cotillo: both are a testimony to illegal building projects that were halted as soon as a new mayor took office. An illegal settlement flourished at a 'finished' construction on the northern coast at Majanicho. North of Caleta de Fustes, a holiday complex *Costa de Antigua* has been built in a no-man's land. Parts of the unfinished resort are empty and simply add to the overall mood of desolation.

Pristine pool, perfect palms: the Hotel Costa Calma Palace

life. As soon as you enter the reception area you will be impressed with its aesthetics. The hotel has its own diving school and *Egli surf school*. Another attraction is the large shady garden with three swimming pools. Entertainment, child care facilities, a spa area and various bars. *Tel. 9 28 54 70 25 | www.solmelia. com/hotels/spain/fuerteventura/melia-gorriones/index.html | Moderate*

SOTAVENTO BEACH CLUB

The resort complex with direct beach access has multiple low-key leisure and entertainment possibilities to choose from. Only some of the spacious 310 apartments have sea views however they all have terraces or balconies. Scuba diving school. *Tel. 9 28 54 70 60 | www.so-taventobeachclub.com | Expensive*

TARO BEACH HOTEL/ MONICA BEACH CLUB

If it is social mingling you are after, then this is the right place for you. Both these terraced hotels are directly on the beach and in the centre there is a large swimming pool area and a bar. Almost all the rooms (*Monica Beach* 410, *Taro Beach* 293) have ocean views and private sun terraces. A communal sports centre offers tennis courts (as well as coaching), table tennis, volleyball and mini golf. There are a number of entertainment possibilities. Guests of the two hotels may use the amenities of both hotels. *Monica Beach: tel. 9 28 54 70 75 | Taro Beach: tel. 9 28 54 70 76 | www.sbhoteles.es | Moderate*

WHERE TO GO

LA PARED
(129 F3) (*Ø B11*)

The narrowest part of the island, the desert-like Istmo de la Pared (isthmus of the wall) is also situated at Costa Calma. One theory is that the wall separated two ancient Canarian kingdoms but there is no evidence to support this. Only a few insignificant remains of the wall have been

The shimmering turquoise waters of the Playa Barca lagoon

found. The La Pared settlement on the west coast has been named after the wall – and it is a place for individualists. You should not come here for its rather odd main road that has hardly any traffic and even less houses. Instead you should pay a visit so that you can try *El Camello*: a great local restaurant *ideal for an al fresco meal*. Their specials must be ordered in advance: *sancocho* with *gofio* for two persons, and *puchero canario* for a minimum of four diners *(closed Mon | right at the first roundabout in La Pared | tel. 9 28 54 90 66 | Budget–Moderate)*.

The Canarian restaurant *Bahía La Pared* offers fresh fish and sea views, beautiful at sunset *(Moderate)*. North of the *barrancos* (ravines) at the end of a path near a rocky outcrop with a section that has been worn by the action of the waves into an arch. During high tide, and if the sea

is rough, the seawater surges up and jets through the opening. The fine sand beach is a good place to linger: small pools are formed by the tide in the shallow sedimentary rocks, little fish swim in the shallows at low tide, sea worms make strange patterns in the sand and the ochre coloured cliffs, black pebbles and reddish sand form changing patterns and contrasts, and above the rock arch the sea foam evaporates into natural salt pans. A special place indeed.

The west coast is ideal for surfing – especially at El Viejo Rey beach. The oldest of the three surf experts is *Waveguru* (formerly *Cowabunga* | tel. 6 19 80 44 47 | www.waveguru.de/en/surfschool-index. html). Surf enthusiasts can also stay here. The stables *Rancho Barranco de los Caballos (tel. 6 19 27 53 89, 9 28 17 41 51)* offers experienced riders INSIDER TIP won-

protected terrace that has views of the distant coast and the ocean. Rice dishes are their speciality . *Wed–Mon from 1pm | right on the road after La Lajita (turn off onto the old road) | tel. 9 28 94 96 95 | Moderate*

PLAYA BARCA ★ ●
(129 E4–5, F4) (*∅ A13/B12*)
This middle section of the sandy beaches, with Costa Calma on the northern end, is the most beautiful part of the Playas de Sotavento. Here, behind a narrow 4km/ 2.4mi long spit of land, is a large lagoon that is mostly dry or easy to wade through during low tide. The spit is often flooded, so be careful that your belongings do not float away! The only large building here is the *Meliá Gorriones* hotel. The Playa Barca is one of the best windsurfing spots in the world and every year in July the world championships take place here.

ESQUINZO/ BUTIHONDO

(129 D6) (*∅ A14*) From the new motorway the Butihondo exit leads to two separate holiday resorts. After the exit you can turn left to the Robinson Club or right to several other large hotel complexes.

derful rides through the beautiful and isolated terrain on the wild western coast. Drive 20.5km/12.7mi on then left on the FV 605 to Pájara. Also deserving of a mention is the *Golf Academy* that offers introductory courses *(see chapter 'Sports & Activities')*.

Coming from Costa Calma on the country road, do not turn left at the town, but take a right and follow the dirt road for 1.4km/0.8mi to *Quesería La Pastora* where you can learn more about the production of goat's cheese and also buy cheese at very affordable prices *(Mon–Sat 8.30am–1.30pm, 4.30pm–6.30pm)*.

MIRADOR DE SOTAVENTO
(130 A–B6) (*∅ C12*)
The mirador (viewing point) is primarily a restaurant – and aptly named. Here you can dine outside on a ● covered, wind-

But if you follow the 'Farmacía' sign immediately to the left the route takes you via the old road to the older part of Esqinzo. Parts of this area are very steep so quite a few of the hotel rooms have wonderful sea views. As the road runs above the resort, the area is very quiet – and even outside of the resort the area is peaceful and remarkably free of the usual hustle and bustle. Buses travel to Morro Jable/ Jandía Playa several times an hour.

ESQUINZO/BUTIHONDO

FOOD & DRINK

MARABÚ

Those who work in the tourism industry in the south, take their guests to this establishment. Everything here is spot on: the atmosphere, the service, the value for money as well as the variety and quality of the food. Traditional island dishes, international dishes, fresh ingredients and good wine. There is also a terrace. *Closed Sun | Calle Bonn straight down the country road | tel. 9 28 54 40 98 | Expensive*

SPORTS & ACTIVITIES

Below the resorts the long Playa de Esquinzo beach stretches out (many nudist beaches). The Robinson Club has a sailing school (with catamarans), a windsurfing school and tennis courts (with coaches). If you are not staying at the club, you can visit *Matchpoint Sports* for all matters concerning tennis *(on artificial grass or clay courts)* and for swimming lessons *(in the garden of the Fuerteventura Princess | tel. 9 28 54 43 07)*.

ENTERTAINMENT

In the old part of Esquinzo, the meeting place is *Safari Bar* at the Monte del Mar swimming pool.

WHERE TO STAY

ESQUINZO/MONTE DEL MAR
The two neighbouring complexes are under the same management. Both are close to the beach and both have a small swimming pool. The *Monte del Mar* even has a small shop and of course the popular *Safari Bar*. The *El Marinero* restaurant has a sheltered wind-free terrace where the Di Meglio family serves a selection of tasty Italian and Canarian dishes, including pizza. *140 units | C. Escanfraga 2 | tel. 9 28 54 40 85 | esquinzo.montedelmar@gmail.com | Moderate*

FUERTEVENTURA PRINCESS/
CLUB JANDÍA PRINCESS
The two large four star resort complexes each comprise of one large main hotel and two-storey units in a garden around a pool area with restaurants and bars. Both impress with their traditional island style with white walls and dark wood. The main building of the *Fuerteventura Princess* hotel is an architectural revelation. The *Jandía Princess* which is run as an all-inclusive club has 528 air-conditioned rooms and the *Fuerteventura Princess* has 715, all with telephone and private balcony or terrace, often with sea views. They also offer tennis courts, a sauna, entertainment and direct beach access. *Fuerteven-*

tura Princess: tel. 9 28 54 41 36 | Jandía Princess: tel. 9 28 54 40 89 | www.princess-hotels.com | Moderate

ROBINSON CLUB ESQUINZO PLAYA

This is the newer of the island's two Robinson Clubs and can accommodate 1000 guests with a focus on families. Their entertainment and child care facilities are ideal and one part of the resort complex is a quiet resting zone. Direct beach access. *Tel. 9 28 16 80 00 | www.robinson.com | Expensive*

WHERE TO GO

DUNES AT RISCO DEL PASO ★
(129 E5) (*𝄞 A13*)

At Risco del Paso (turn off the country road on to an asphalt road at 71.8km/45mi) the Playa Barca lagoon ends. The attractions of this little stretch of beach – one of the most beautiful on the whole island – are its two small sand dunes and its grassy knolls and secluded little hollows. Quite a number of nudists. The sea in front of Risco del Paso is a favourite surf spot and it is also where you'll find René Egli.

MORRO JABLE/ JANDÍA PLAYA

(128 C6) (*𝄞 C–D3*) This village at the most southern tip of Fuerteventura is the largest tourist centre on the island and it consists of two very different parts.

Straight out of a construction kit: the centre of Morro Jable

MORRO JABLE/JANDÍA PLAYA

Morro Jable (or Morro del Jable) is not very old yet it is a traditional harbour village in a very beautiful location. East of it, on the other side of a hill, which is now built up, hotels and apartment complexes make up the large holiday resorts that have come to be known as Jandía Playa

The beach promenade which starts at the Robinson Club and leads up to Morro Jable and the popular fish restaurants is small, quiet, full of atmosphere and right next to the water. The simplicity and authentic Spanish nature of the old part of Morro Jable offers an interesting contrast

No matter where you stay – there is always a sea view

or Jandía. The official name is *Solana de Matorral* or *Solana de Jandía*. Its beach is the *Playa de Matorral*.

Jandía Playa essentially consists of a leafy main road with many terraced hotel and apartment complexes built down its slope. Here there are numerous bars, restaurants and shops. So much so that there is now a promenade that links *Stella Canaris* in the east with the old *Cosmo* shopping centre in the west. The promenade is particularly busy at night. Opposite the promenade is a protected salt marsh and behind it the beach.

to the artificial, large-scale holiday resorts in its immediate neighbourhood.

Thanks to the fact that the resorts are built on terraced hillsides, you can almost always expect to have a room with a sea view and will of course also be right close to the sea. However, you will still need to cross the main road and the salt marsh in order to access the beach (with a few exceptions). Today, Jandía Playa is expanding more towards the north-east, where the streets no longer run right next to the coast so the new houses there all have direct beach access.

FOOD & DRINK

If you do not mind the trip, then you can have a lovely intimate lunch (or dinner) in Morro Jable. There on the beach promenade you will be able to dine better than at the restaurants on the main road at Jandía Playa. In Morro Jable the restaurants all offer a very similar menu choice and the quality and standards are all on par with each other. The usual combination of fresh fish, tasty *papas arrugadas* and a sea view keeps guests very happy. However, if taste is more important than the view, you should rather go to one of the restaurants behind the promenade, where the meals are often better, and certainly cheaper.

Morro's two small main roads are not geared towards tourism so if you want to visit the bars or restaurants there it would help if you speak some Spanish. Of the various cafés and ice-cream parlours, these three are the best and they all happen to be run by German expats: the *Café Caracola* with its bakery *(C. Bardino, other side of the Avda. Saladar behind the Hotel Buganvilla)*, the *Eisdealer (at the Avda. Saladar a few steps towards the west)* and the *Eiscafé Magdalena (Avda. Saladar 22 D, on the hill at the petrol station)*.

INSIDER TIP **CORONADO** ☺

The cuisine on offer here is very upmarket and the menu stands out with its delicious combinations that blend Canarian, Mediterranean and Asian influences. The majority of the ingredients are sourced locally from the island – and you can certainly taste freshness and the difference in quality. Reasonable prices and good portions. If you linger at the bar after dinner, you may meet the senior chef – a great source of information about the pioneering days of tourism on the island. *Thu–Tue, evenings only | next to the Riu*

Palace Jandía | tel. 9 28 54 11 74 | Moderate–Expensive

FAROLA DEL MAR

This is where you should go for the best fish in the area – with a terrace and a sea view. *Closed Wed | in Morro Jable at the steps to the new church behind the Laja restaurant | tel. 9 28 54 08 34 | Moderate*

MATTARELLO

Good Italian close to the promenade down in Morro Jable. Elegantly furnished dining room but most guests prefer to sit outside and watch the sea. Many classic dishes are served (pizza, pasta, etc.) but with a creative twist. *Closed Mon | Avda. Tomas Grau Gurrea 2 | tel. 9 28 54 08 04 | Budget–Moderate*

PICCOLA ITALIA

This restaurant has its own classic stone oven and serves the most delicious wood-fired pizzas. *Closed Thu | C. del Carmen 39 | tel. 9 28 54 12 58 | Budget*

STETSON

Those dining in this popular restaurant (which is situated in the rather ugly CC Cosmo) should rather focus on the food and not worry about the surroundings. Delicious steaks and other meat dishes, but also good fish, pizza and much more. *Only Sun–Fri evenings | CC Cosmo, upper floor | tel. 9 28 16 63 59 | Moderate*

SHOPPING

The main road has a good selection of diverse shops and there are some bargains to be had shopping in the 80 odd shops down in Morro Jable. Approaching from Jandía you will reach the large supermarket *Padilla* on the right of the street going to the valley (before the turn to the left). Don't forget that Thursday is market day on the main road at the open space next to CC Cosmo.

ACTIVITIES & SPORT

ACTIVITIES IN THE HARBOUR

There are quite a few to choose from and many of them are under one roof at *Excursiones Náuticas (tel. 6 90 96 59 01 | www.excursiones-nauticas.com):* jet ski, banana boats, speed boats, waterskis, wakeboarding and deep sea fishing. The almost two hour long jet ski ride to the western cape can also be booked directly on *tel. 6 16 43 71 84.* For sport fishing you can also take the *Blue Nose (tel. 6 28 02 14 51)* out.

For sun, swimming and snorkelling, take the *MS Blue Bird (tel. 9 28 16 69 93)* to sea. Sail boats mean enjoyable trips (without engine noise) and can be booked through the tour guide in the hotel. Two examples are the *Magic* and *Santa María* catamarans and the two-mast *Pedra Sartaña* built in 1940, that takes to sea on Tuesdays to Saturdays for a pirate tour while you can book a INSIDER TIP diving trip for dives of up to 30m/99ft on *Subcat (tel. 9 28 16 63 92).*

BICYCLES

Fuertebike hires out bicycles and organises tours *(tel. 6 29 36 27 95, Uli |www.fuerte bike.com/english.html).* At *Jandía Patines* one can rent normal bicycles as well as four-wheel pedal bikes by the hour *(wooden shed at the western end of the salt marsh | tel. 6 80 57 43 83).*

MOTORBIKE, TRIKE & QUAD BIKE TRIPS

Trips through the area on dirt bikes and quads are offered by *Sahara Sports (tel. 6 06 60 00 90).* INSIDER TIP Trike tours can be undertaken at *Fuerte Trike (CC Cosmo | in the internet café in the base-*ment | tel. 9 28 16 63 01).* Scooters and quads are available at *Montes Quads (C. Estrella del Mar, at the CC Faro | tel. 9 28 16 66 70).*

SAILING & SURFING

The main providers in the area are the water sport centre on the beach side of the *Robinson Club (tel. 9 28 16 95 39).* Below the *Club Aldiana, Surfers Island* not only offers windsurfing and ● catamaran sailing but also surfing and kayak trips *(tel. 6 90 26 52 55 | or through Aldiana: tel. 9 28 16 98 70, ext. 119).*

BEACHES & SWIMMING

Even during high season, the almost 50m/ 164ft wide fine golden sand Jandía Playa *(Playa de Matorral)* beach, is never crowded but renting two loungers and an umbrella will cost you a rather hefty 9 euro per day. Nude bathing close to the town is frowned upon. For swimming lessons you can go to *Matchpoint (tel. 6 29 06 78 68).*

SCUBA DIVING

The most reputable and well established diving school in the area is *Felix (Jandía Playa | next to CC Faro in the main road | tel. 9 28 54 14 18).*

TENNIS

The better hotels offer artificial grass and clay courts. Lessons at *Matchpoint (tel. 6 69 45 81 68).*

ENTERTAINMENT

The focal point is in the area between Stella Canaris and CC Faro, the CC Cosmo with neighbouring CC Palm Garden and the seaside end of Morro Jable. In Stella Canaris, the ● *Cervezería Olimpo* is popular because of its spacious patio and aside from the usual beer *(cerveza)* they also serve some great cocktails. In the CC Palm

Garden, the *Bar Oasis* is the main attraction. They have a live band, a dance floor and the cocktails are top class and a few hundred feet further along in the CC Cosmo, a loyal (mostly German) crowd enjoy their chilled beers in the *Bar Eskimo*. On weekends a small but notable live

In Morro you can also experience Los Rodríguez (also known as the Morro City Band) a great four-man ensemble.
The discos really only start filling up after midnight: the *Noche Tropical (CC Cosmo)* and the *Mafasca* at the Stella Canaris *(left through the south entrance at the rear).*

A real pirate adventure: sailing on the Atlantic

music scene unfolds. Many music-loving hotel employees turn into band members. The *Strings* in the upper floor of the CC Cosmo is one such venue and is operated by enthusiastic amateurs. Things are a little louder and hipper in INSIDERTIP *La Tortuga* when Sopa de Tortuga start up around midnight with ska and reggae *(east end of CC Faro, upper floor).* Those who like Spanish music, should visit *San Borondón* in Morro Jable where young and old, Spaniards and locals and (some) tourists come together over beers and tapas and to enjoy the proprietor's music.

WHERE TO STAY

In Jandía Playa accommodation options are mainly in large hostel complexes. If you prefer accommodation with a more personal atmosphere, you should go to Morro Jable.

APARTAMENTOS ALBERTO

20 apartments with sea views that are simply but adequately equipped. *Avda. del Faro 4 | Morro Jable | tel. 9 28 54 51 09 | www.aptosalberto.com | Budget (without breakfast)*

MORRO JABLE/JANDÍA PLAYA

AQUAMARIN

17 rooms (some spacious) with private balconies or terraces, a swimming pool and in a quiet area. Good value for money. *C. Flamenco 2 (in the valley next to Stella Canaris) | tel. 9 28 54 03 24 | www. aquamarin.com | Moderate*

ATALAYA DE JANDÍA

This exquisite complex seems to be suspended above the sea and is right in the

del Faro 8 | on the slope above Morro Jable | tel. 9 28 54 17 44 | www.apartamentos-casablanca.com | Moderate

CLUB ALDIANA

In the spacious park-like complex with direct beach access you can choose between the hotel wing and the bungalows (361 units, many with sea views) which are ideal for those guests looking for some peace and quiet. Children are also

The perfect conditions for windsurfing

front of the rocks in the west of Morro Jable, above the church. The 20 spacious, well-equipped apartments have their own balconies and the complex also has a small swimming pool. *C. Los Guanches 46 | tel. 9 28 54 02 27 | Expensive*

CASABLANCA

Small complex run by Germans, with 13 well-equipped apartments or studios (with sea view). Small swimming pool. *Avda.*

well looked after. In addition to the usual amenities like restaurants, shops, disco, swimming pool etc., there is also a surf and sailing school, scuba diving courses, a fitness studio, golf coaches, bicycle rentals, squash, tennis and more. No other resort in Jandia combines the assets of the island as well as this one. Rest and exercise, solitude and companionship, nature and culture are all in perfect harmony. *Valle de Butihondo, at the end*

of the motorway | tel. 9 28 16 98 70 |
Expensive

FARO JANDÍA
A centrally located vibrant hotel and a good choice for those who like to do things outside of the hotel. The 214 rooms (all with own balcony, many with sea views) are air-conditioned. The hotel has a swimming pool, fitness centre, tennis courts and mini golf. The large well-run spa area *Las Caricias del Faro* has a wide range of facilities like a swimming pool, sauna, Turkish bath, massages, and a diverse array of beauty treatments. You do not have to be a guest of the hotel to use the spa *(tel. 9 28 16 70 74). Avda. del Saladar lighthouse | tel. 9 28 54 50 35 | www.mur hoteles.com | Expensive*

RIU PALACE JANDÍA
The majority of the 201 spacious rooms offer great views over the beach however, the swimming pool area is very narrow and there are many steps. You can glide down to the beach in a glass lift. *Jandía Playa | tel. 9 28 54 03 70 | www.riu.com | Expensive*

ROBINSON CLUB JANDÍA PLAYA
The palm-lined resort with swimming pool – and everything else that you might expect from a club in this price range – is the only one situated in the flat foreshore on the beach. In 2010 they celebrated their 40th anniversary and this is also the oldest of all the Robinson Clubs. The club is great for young couples and singles – the club in Esquinzo is better suited to families with children. The 362 rooms are divided between the air-conditioned hotel and the two-storied building in the large garden. Sporting activities on offer include tennis, scuba diving and windsurfing. *Jandía Playa on the main road | tel. 9 28 16 91 00 | www.robinson.com | Expensive (full board)*

STELLA CANARIS HOTELS & RESORT
The largest hotel, apartment and bungalow resort on the island is like a city itself and stretches from the coast road into a side valley and up the hillside. The 1000 units (approx.), all with telephone, are divided into five different complexes of bungalows, apartments and hotels. Its proximity to the beach – with entrance through a tunnel underneath the main road – the huge palm garden with zoo, various swimming pools as well as special entertainment for young guests, make this resort a paradise for families with children of all ages. The atmosphere is very lively. In addition there is also soccer,

ALTERNATIVE PLACE NAMES

Something as official as a place name should be constant, one would think. This is not the case in Fuerteventura. Instead of Morro Jable one can also say Morro del Jable, you can say Vega de Río de las Palmas or Vega de Río Palma. The holiday resort in the bay Caleta de Fustes completely confuses with its six different names: for instance Costa Caleta, Playa de Castillo, Catillo de Fuste or El Castillo ... Many places have an article in front of the name like La Antigua or La Oliva, but it is often simply omitted. The listings in this are done according to the latter.

tennis, squash, a disco and much more. Although there are three lifts to help negotiate the differences in height, those who are not as steady on their feet or families with prams, should rather stay in the part of the resort situated in the valley. *Jandía Playa on the main road | tel. 9 28 87 33 99 | www.stellacanaris.es | Budget–Moderate*

OFICINA DE TURISMO
In the basement of the CC Cosmo | Mon–Fri 9am–3pm | tel. 9 28 54 07 76

Road to Cofete

WHERE TO GO

PICO DE LA ZARZA ☀
(128 C5–6) (⑳ C2)
At 807m/2647.6ft this is the highest summit on the island and is also known as *Pico de Jandía*. Only accessible by foot, it is an almost three hour climb. At the beginning and the end of the hike there are some very steep sections but in between there are some less demanding stretches. The hike as such is not very difficult. Normal walking shoes should do – sandals are definitely not an option. Once you have found the entrance point, you cannot get lost as the path has been walked many times so it is easy to identify. When the summit is not surrounded by trade wind clouds, the view from the top is quite overwhelming. Increase your chances of a clear view by hiking up in the morning rather than in the afternoon. The starting point is at the large roundabout at the Jandía Playa village entrance, where the country road and the salt marsh meet. Take the wide road past *CC Ventura* and the hotel *Barceló Jandía Playa*. Just behind the hotel, you turn left and after about 600m/1970ft turn right into a cul-de-sac at the end of which is a building that you have to walk around. Now you only need to follow the track. At about 700m/2300ft you will reach the fence that surrounds the summit area in order to keep out hungry goats. At this height the trade wind clouds provide enough precipitation so that protected plants thrive between the rocks. In order to protect these plants for the future, please ensure that you close the gate behind you. From here a narrow, winding path leads steeply up to the ridge, follow the ridge to the right to reach the summit.

You hike should take about five hours under normal conditions and walking at a moderate pace. You should bear in mind that there is no food available along the way and of course you should take enough water along. At the top you will have to reckon with strong winds and you should take something warm along to wear. Just as important is good sun protection (hat and sunscreen), because there is no shade.

WESTERN CAPE AND COFETE ★ ●

The extreme western tip of the island, the Punta de Jandía, is often falsely referred to as the south cape, when Morro Jable is clearly more southern. The trip to Punta de Jandía, over a dusty bumpy road is still quite a bit of an adventure – an off-road vehicle is the best option. There are a few destinations worth visiting here. There is the little fishing village *Puerto de la Cruz* (128 A6) *(⌖ A3)* which has three pubs that all serve fresh seafood. There is an exhibition in the nearby lighthouse, which runs on solar energy, giving more information about local marine life *(Tue–Sun 10.30am–5.30pm)*. On a clear day you can see Gran Canaria from here.

Cofete (128 C5) *(⌖ C2)* the most remote town on the island consists of a few houses and shacks that use their own generators for electricity and there is no running water. The few remaining inhabitants live off goat farming and the tourists that visit the Bar Cofete for its fish soup *(Moderate)*. The main attraction however, is the Villa Winter surrounded as it is in a shroud of mystery. More about this as well as the stretch in between in the chapter 'Trips & Tours', trip no. 3.

There is also the option to walk to Cofete on one of the INSIDER TIP old royal roads *(camino reales)*. From there drive 3.2km/ 1.9mi from the harbour to *Gran Valle*, where you can walk from the car park (signposted: Red de Caminos de Pájara) keep going straight up the valley. The road is being revamped and you cannot get lost. There and back should take about two hours, so take some snacks and water along. ☆ There is a wonderful view from the mountain saddle.

Shrouded in mystery: Villa Winter

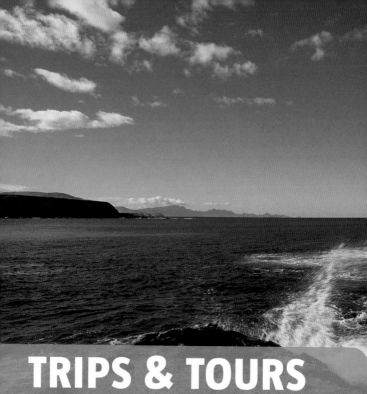

TRIPS & TOURS

The tours are marked in green in the road atlas, the pull-out map and on the back cover

1 HIGHLIGHTS OF THE NORTH: LAVA, VILLAGES, DUNES

The tour takes you through lava landscapes and dunes, to the holy mountain Tindaya past the rugged west coast and to the island's capital. An outdoor museum offers insights into the life of the Majoreros, the indigenous islanders. 135km/84mi 7 hours.

The trip starts in the western region of Corralejo → p. 32 and runs along a winding track to a small bay and the saltwater desalination plant, over a barren and an inhospitable stretch of land strewn with lava rocks. The stony desert landscape (Malpaís) are as a result of volcanic eruptions that took place between 10,000 to 4000 years ago. In some places, white sand has settled between the black rocks creating some remarkable contrast. In Majanicho a wide track branches off to the south and leads to Lajares → p. 42, an arts and crafts centre. Turn right at the roundabout on the old country road, this section goes through fields covered with lava rocks and leads to Cotillo.

Cotillo → p. 40 is famous for its fish restaurants. The southern edge of the village has a defence tower, lime kilns, a new harbour and a mini promenade and this

Photo: Rocky coast at Puerto de la Peña/Ajuy

Explore the island's adventurous roads in a rental car or on foot and uncover its hidden nooks and crannies

is where you get your first impression of the rugged west coast. Next you travel along the FV 10 to La Oliva → p. 44, the island's northern capital, the seat of its administration and home to the contemporary art centre, the *Centro de Arte Canario*. From Oliva head south-west towards the red Montaña Tindaya → p. 45, once sacred to the island's original inhabitants.

From Tindaya on the FV 10 further to the south, you will pass the Montaña Quemada → p. 46 with the statue of the poet Miguel de Unamuno. Shortly after that the FV 207 road branches to the right to Tefía, a small farming settlement with the interesting La Alcogida outdoor museum → p. 102 where you can get a glimpse of how the islanders used to live before you take a break.

A bit further south, turn right at the sign-post and take the road to *Puertito de los Molinos*. On the right hand side, behind the restored mill, you will see the old landing strip where the first passenger plane landed in 1950. In the settlement of *Las Parcelas* (5.9km/3.6mi from the country road) a gravel road curves to the right and then branches to the left and leads to the Embalse de los Molinos resevoir, the dam which was built in 1940. It is 102m/334ft long and 42m/138ft high making it the largest on the island. It was built to irrigate the fields but as it is often empty, it has never been able to fulfil its original purpose.

Now it is time to go back to the coast, to ● INSIDERTIP *Puertito de los Molinos*, the 'small mill harbour'. The smallest fishing village on the island looks rundown and has unsurfaced roads, but despite this quite a number of wealthy citizens from the island's capital have weekend homes here. You can only get to the village by crossing a small bridge or a footbridge. The *barranco* has a permanently flowing stream that feeds into a duck pond, and in one spot there is also a shrine to the Mother and Child decorated in a folk art style by the fishermen in honour of their patron saint. The village bar and restaurant *Casa Pon* has a terrace and is a good place to recharge. From the small parking lot in front of the village (or on the beach) a foot path climbs up to a 🌊 viewing point on the rocks: a great place to experience the spray of the waves breaking along the rugged west coast. Back on the main road, head south through the church village Casillas del Ángel → p. 52 and on to Puerto del Rosario → p. 47 where a short walk through the city is recommended.

Now go back along the coastal road FV 1, which passes the holiday resort *Parque Holandés*, to the highlight of the trip, the

Typical flowering cacti and colonial architecture in Antigua

magnificent dunes at **El Jable** → p. 34 and then again back to Corralejo.

2 TO BETANCURIA AND THE MOUNTAINS

This tour takes you through the island's mountainous centre (with some great vantage points), and to the most historically, and culturally, important places in the Canary Islands. 140km/87mi approx. 7 hours.

Coming from the holiday resorts in the south, you first pass the tomato cultivation region and then come to **Tuineje** → p. 69 the smallest of the island's old villages. In the village church you can view the altar that depicts the battle of Tamacite. In the north is **Tiscamanita** and its **mill museum** → p. 69. If you are driving an off-road vehicle go past the Tio Pepe bar and turn off to the right, onto a road 3.9km/2.4mi to the east (left at the fork in the road) a short way past the power line turn right, and you will come the edge of the **Malpaís Grande**. The trip ends halfway up the volcanic cone ☼ **Caldera de la Laguna** (that is layered with volcanic ash) where you get a panoramic view of the island. The dark lunarscape of the lava fields – the large one to the right is the **Malpaís Chico** stands out against the lighter older land. Next up is **Antigua** → p. 55 with its traditional craftwork and exhibition centre north of the town. From Antigua take the FV 416 that leads first through flat plains, and then heads steeply uphill. From the ☼ top of the **Tegú** → p. 59 pass you will have a great view of the north of the island. Now the road heads steeply downwards to **Betancuria** → p. 58. The former capital is the most important travel destination of the interior and has a ruined monastery, church, museums and lots of arts and

crafts. Here you can dine in the beautiful *Casa Santa María* before heading south to the palm oasis **Vega de Río de las Palmas** → p. 59 where you should go for a hike through the rocky **Barranco de las Peñitas** gorge. Back in the car the road now goes straight up to the next pass with a wonderful view of the mountains and valleys. Then the descent goes to the south to **Pájara** → p. 65 famous for its church with its Mexican façade and beautiful altars. Leave the village via the FV 605 and take the side road FV 621, which runs past a valley full of palm trees to the fishing village **Ajuy/Puerto de la Peña** → p. 67. Walking from the black sand beach (with beach bar) you get to the sea caves in just a few minutes.

Back on the FV 605 (to the right) the road takes you through an uninhabited and isolated mountainous region. If the haze is not too thick, you can see all along the Jandía peninsula from the **Tablada** mountain pass. It is worth a climb up the hill east (left) of the road – when the sun sets, the colour of the stones change remarkably.

3 FROM THE EAST COAST TO VILLA WINTER ★

Although the majority of this tour is on surfaced roads, it is far better to do it in an off-road vehicle as almost 70km/44mi of the route is on unsurfaced roads. The starting point for this trip is Caleta de Fuste, but if you are staying on the Jandía peninsula you can take a short cut. The stretch including the return trip (without the detour over Pozo Negro or any other detours) is 231km/143mi long.

From Caleta de Fustes drive 3.5km/2mi to the south, then turn left to **Salinas del Carmen** → p. 63. The road leads you straight up to the salt museum with scattered piles of sea salt that glitter in the sun. The street that passes at the top of the town turns into a track that leads downhill to the mouth of the surprisingly green **Barranco de la Torre**. A small winding road heads back uphill. The next short stretch is through some completely isolated desert terrain. After crossing another small barranco you will come to a fork in the road. The road to the right is longer and more comfortable while the road ahead has more curves and is very steep in parts. Both roads join up again. At **Pozo Negro** → p. 57 the road is once again surfaced. After travelling 2.8km/ 1.7mi on the FV 420, turn left on to a track that leads to the ancient ruins **La Atalayita** → p. 57. Now back to the FV 402 and left (inland) and then left again at the junction to the FV 2. The next destination on the route is Gran Tarajal and (just as at La Atalayita) it takes you through some rugged lava fields. You need not spend too much time in **Gran Tarajal** → p. 65, but try to make some time to

enjoy a coffee or a cool drink on the spacious promenade to take in the peaceful atmosphere that characterises this little village.

Next you travel 21km/13mi to **Oasis Park** → p. 69, p. 103 at La Lajita, but it would be better to visit the zoo, cactus garden and animal performances on the way back or on another day when you have more time to do some sightseeing as it is still quite a distance to get to the furthest destination, the western cape and Villa Winter. Do not miss out on a detour to the **Playa Barca lagoon** → p. 79 (5.5km/ 3.4mi after Costa Calma turn to the left), and you should also make time for a stop in **Morro Jable** → p. 81 possibly for lunch with a view of the sea. You have now reached the most southern point of the island.

This next part includes the best off-road terrain on the island as the road to the western tip of the Jandía peninsula always has a whiff of adventure to it. On your way there it is better to travel around

The lighthouse between Morro Jable and Jandía Playa is on the most southern tip of the island

Morro Jable on the bypass road. Just before you reach the harbour, turn right at the signposted road and drive for 20km/ 12.4mi towards the coast. This section of road is through barren semi-desert landscapes. Just before your destination of **Punta de Jandía** – a narrow headland that juts into the sea crowned with a lighthouse – lies the small village of **Puerto de la Cruz → p. 89**.

From Puerto de la Cruz there is also another detour you can take: opposite the *Punta Jandía* restaurant is a narrow asphalt road that turns north to ☀ **Punta Pesebre**. On the right hand side of the road, you will see the old landing strip that runs parallel to the road.

Drive back to the junction where a mountain pass leads to the north coast and to Cofete. Soon you will reach **Roque del Moro**, the most beautiful ☀ view point in the southern part of the island (watch out, the wind can easily blow items right out of your car or your hat from your head!). Stretching down below is the white sandy

Playa de Cofete beach which is bordered in the east by the small 'island' **El Islote**. Behind it the wide beach of **Playa de Barlovento** can be seen and on a clear day you will be able to see the mountains of Pàjara in the north-east. From the beaches the hillsides slope up to **Pico de Jandía** (also Pico de la Zarza), with the highest mountain peak (807m/2647.6ft) on the island. On the slopes are some large and unusual plants, candelabra-shaped shrubs, which resemble cacti.

The next village is **Cofete → p. 89**. Even before you reach this rather bleak little settlement, you will immediately notice the isolated double storey house, with its round tower, on the slope. This is the mysterious and fabled **Villa Winter**. You can only reach it by foot or in an off-road vehicle. According to legend, the German engineer Gustav Winter (1893–1971) leased the whole peninsula in 1937 so that the German navy could establish a submarine harbour here. Two German islanders have subsequently undertaken numerous archival studies and investigations and have proven the story to be just as unlikely as all the other myths that surround the old house (the 'Fuerte Fan Magazine' published the research results in 2005–07). The building was never completely finished and was not regularly occupied. However, under Franco control of the peninsula went to 'Don Gustavos' (Winter) who ruled over his massive hacienda like a feudal lord. In 1964 it was divided into four parts and was sold off. Today the villa is occupied by goat herders and regular viewings are not possible, but a small fee might help open its doors for a tour. However there really are no hidden secrets to uncover.

Steer clear of a trip along the endless sandy beaches. Crossing the nature reserve is strictly prohibited and if you are caught you will be heavily fined.

SPORTS & ACTIVITIES

Lazing on the beach in the sun for two weeks? Thanks to Fuerteventura's wide selection of sporting activities, it would be a shame to spend your holiday just lounging around. The most popular activities are all the various water sports, with windsurfing being on top due to ideal trade winds. But there are also lots of options for the less energetic.

Addresses of sports companies not listed below, can be found under the 'Sports & Activities' section for the individual towns. The expression, 'in all the large holiday resorts' refers to: Corralejo, Caleta de Fustes, Costa Calma/La Pared and Jandía Playa/Morro Jable.

BICYCLES & MOTORBIKES

INSIDER TIP Cycling is very popular sport and there are rentals available at all the large holiday resorts like Taralejo and Las Playitas. They often also have organised mountain bike trips in varying degrees of difficulty, most of them are not too demanding and you can piggyback and be motor powered uphill and then free wheel downhill. If you prefer to experience the island under your own steam you should avoid the main roads where possible. A bicycle network is currently under construction. Motorcycle trips with dirt bikes or quad bikes are also available

This is an island that is ideal for water sports lovers: it is a paradise for swimmers, divers, surfers, windsurfers and kiteboarders

in all the large holiday resorts. In the south you can book through *Sahara Sports* (Morro Jable) and there are also companies in Taralejo.

FISHING

You do not need a licence to fish on Fuerteventura and can do so from piers or from the rocks. The necessary equipment can be purchased quite reasonably in Puerto del Rosario or Corralejo. Calamari, shrimp and small crabs are used as bait. There are minimum sizes prescribed for any fish that you catch. A more exciting option is to go on a deep sea fishing trip. There are companies in Corralejo, Costa Calma and Morro Jable that do boat trips and they also provide all the necessary equipment.

Putting on Salinas de Antigua's lush green golf course

GOLF

Golf took off on the island in 2002 when the 18-hole course at Caleta de Fustes was opened (par 70, with driving range, putting green, etc., *tel. 9 28 16 00 34*). Today there are two additional 18-hole courses *Salinas de Antigua* and *Las Playitas*, the latter is part of the sport centre *Playitas Grand Resort*. There are also two smaller facilities: *Mirador de Lobos Golf* on the outskirts of Corralejo and the well-established *golf academy* in La Pared, with a six-hole course, driving range and practice course *(tel. 9 28 54 91 03)*. Holiday clubs and some hotels also offer driving ranges and putting greens. The Morro Jable golf course is closed (at the time of going to press).

HIKING

For anyone who is interested in nature and the traditional lifestyle of the islanders, the island interior has some interesting surprises. The hike through the Barranco de las Peñitas is thoroughly explained in Vega de Río de las Palmas, so you can easily manage it on your own. It gets really exciting when you take a ⭐ ● *guided hike* with an English speaking guide. They will have fascinating insights about the local flora, fauna, history and geography. *Bookings at the travel agents in the hotels*

HORSERIDING

The number of stables offering rides has shrunk and currently the best choice is the ranch INSIDERTIP *Rancho* at La Pared → p. 78. Their rides out into the wide open space of the rugged west coast give one a true feeling of Fuerteventura adventure and freedom *(tel. 6 19 27 53 89 and 9 28 17 41 51)*.

SAILING

You can learn to sail on catamarans at the *Club Aldiana* at Jandía Playa, the

Robinson Clubs of Esquinzo and Jandía Playa and in Las Playitas. If you just want to relax on a yacht it can be arranged in Corralejo, Morro Jable/Jandía Playa as well as Tarajalejo and Caleto de Fustes. For skippers: there are yacht marinas in Caleta de Fustes, Corralejo and Morro Jable.

SCUBA DIVING

⭐ *Scuba diving* in Feurtaventura is a lot of fun and dive sites like the El Río straits at Corralejo, the moray eel reef in front of Jandía Playa and various other spots are all popular. The island's lava formations and diverse marine treasures make it one of the best diving areas in the Canaries. Scuba diving schools are based in all the large holiday resorts as well as Las Playitas. To learn to dive you first need a medical certificate but there are a number of local doctors who provide this service.

TENNIS

Good hotels and clubs have artificial grass and clay courts but some may only have concrete courts or insufficient protection against the wind. Lessons are offered in various hotels in the south by *Matchpoint Sports (tel. 6 69 45 81 68)*.

WATERSKI, JET SKI & BANANA BOATS

The two-seater jet skis need no introduction and at about 40 euro for 20 minutes, they can be both an expensive and a noisy ride. To get the best jet ski value for money try the companies in the harbour at Morro Jable. Companies that offer jet skis often also rent out banana boats so if you don't feel like driving you can have just as much fun being towed along on a banana boat. There are jet ski companies in Corralejo, Caleta de Fustes and Morro Jable. The majority of them also offer waterskiing.

WINDSURFING & SURFING

⭐ *Windsurfing* is the main water sport on the island. The wind and water conditions are ideal with the strongest wind blowing during the summer. The lowest wind speeds – with occasional lulls – are from November to January. Whether you're a beginner, advanced or an ace there will be just the right spot for you on Fuerteventura. The most important spots are the Playas de Sotavento on the Jandía peninsula, the area around Corralejo and – only for the experts – the beaches in El Cotillo. Surf schools and equipment rentals can be found in all the large holiday resorts.

INSIDER TIP ▶ Kitesurfing is also a very trendy sport and popular spots are Corralejo's dune beach of as well as on Playa Barca in the south. Kitesurfers use a surfboad combined with a large kite that functions as a sail, the board is powered by the wind.

Surf sites for normal surfboarders are along the west coast. There are surf companies in Corralejo *(like Quiksilver | tel. 9 28 86 73 07)* or in Costa Calma/La Pared *(Waveguru | tel. 6 19 80 44 47)*.

The innovative owner of *Otro Modo Surfschool* came up with the wonderful idea of combining surfing with Spanish lessons. There are surf spots with accommodation in bungalows or apartments at Costa Calma and Morro Jable. So while your body takes a rest your brain can get busy with a conversation course. The language classes take place in small groups *(www.otro-modo-surfschool.com | tel. 3 46 75 17 00 04)*.

TRAVEL WITH KIDS

There are numerous possibilities for children of all ages to experience something fun and exciting on Fuerteventura. Most hotels, apartments and resort complexes are geared towards families and children and offer all kinds of entertainment. They cater across the range from affordable, self-catering apartments for the budget-conscious all the way up to the holiday clubs, where professional entertainers keep the children busy all (or almost all) of the time.

Experiencing the island's nature usually ranks right up at the top for children. In places like Puertito de los Molinos, where there are some good vantage points on the rocky coast, the sea with its crashing waves and spray makes for a magnificent spectacle. The island's wonderful sandy beaches and the joy of swimming in the sea is a priceless pleasure for every child. Having said that, a word of warning: it is best not to holiday on the island during spring or summer when gusting winds often whip up the sand making a visit to the beach unsuitable for small children. This is also when the summer sun is at its harshest and not ideal for small children. The south of the island and Caleta de Fustes are both good areas for children as bathing is safe all year round. An accommodation option that is particularly child-friendly is

The island has a lot to offer children – whether it is the beach, go-carting, camel riding, the zoo or the aquarium – they are bound to have fun

Stella Canaris in Jandía Playa. The large and shady resort complex, with its own zoo, has a lot to offer. In Caleta de Fustes the *Barceló Castillo Beach Resort* is the best choice. The accommodation is at ground level, they offer some good entertainment options and the complex is right on a beach that has calm shallow surf, that you can look out over. The *Apartment Hotel des Playitas Grand Resort* in Las Playitas is also a good choice for families with children as they also have a Kids Sports Academy with an entertainment emphasis on sport. The same goes for the *Robinson Club* in Esquinzo. But of course many other hotels on the island offer suitable entertainment options.

Many scuba diving schools also offer scuba diving courses for children who already know how to swim. The companies that

offering views of the world under the sea. During the cruise there is not much to see, but once the boat stops you can feed the fish and it is really quite beautiful *(from 18 euro, children from 9 euro)*.

From Caleta de Fustes (127 E3) *(∭ G8)* a semi-submarine offers the same option *(20 euro, children 10 euro)*. In the *Oceanarium* you can also experience the fish and sea lions up close. At Morro Jable you can dive up to 30m/100ft deep with the submarine 'Sub Cat'.

THE NORTH

OUTDOOR MUSEUM
LA ALCOGIDA ★ ● (126 B1) *(∭ E6)*

The eco-museum in Tefía is one of the largest outdoor museums on the island. It consists of seven restored farms where the rooms are furnished as they were almost one hundred years ago, showing what a household looked like and how people would have lived. A cinema shows films with farmers and their wives baking bread and dyeing. On two of the farms they have also faithfully reproduced some workshops. Children enjoy the *Casa Señor Teodosio* the most as is has a *gofio* mill with a donkey turning the capstan wheel. There are also other animals for the children to see. One house further along they demonstrate how bread is baked in a wood oven and you can watch the whole process starting from when the flour is sieved. The audio guide is very informative *(audio-guía 3 euro)*. Car park and the cashier are located west of the street. *Tue–Sat 10am–6pm | at southern end of town | admission 5 euro*

CAMEL RIDES (123 E2) *(∭ H2)*

The *camel safaris* at the Corralejo dunes are a new activity. The trip starts at the beach near the Hotel Ríu Oliva Beach. A roundtrip on these 'ships of the desert'

A child all dressed up for some carnival fun

offer the courses are in Corralejo and in Morro Jable/Jandía Playa. Children can also expend some energy and jump on the trampoline in Corralejo (next to the Cepsa petrol station at the top of the main road) and in the playground at Caleta de Fustes. Mini-golf is offered at Corralejo at the *Stella Canaris* and the *Faro Jandia* in Jandía Playa (also for non-guests) or at the *Barceló Fuerteventura* in Caleta de Fustes.

THE WHOLE ISLAND

INSIDER TIP BOAT TRIPS

At Corralejo there are cruises on the motorised catamaran 'Celia Cruz' which has underwater windows (123 E1) *(∭ G2)*

takes about 20 minutes. *Daily 11am–5pm | adults 6 euro, children 5 euro*

THE CENTRE

GO-CART TRACK OCIOS DEL SUR
(130 B4) (*ᗰ C10*)

There are three tracks (125m, 500m and 1500m long) as well as a cafeteria for refreshments. *Daily 11am–7pm, during summer 11am–8pm | 10 min 15 euro, youth 10 euro, children 7 euro | approach from the FV 618 that goes south to Cardón (turn left at the go-cart sign)*

OASIS PARK ★ (130 B5) (*ᗰ C12*)

Chimpanzees, otters, kangaroos, hippos, ostriches, marabou storks, flamingos, giraffes and other animals are all part of the attraction of this amazing park. Do not miss out on the entertaining animal shows with reptiles, parrots, sea lions and birds of prey. *Daily 9am–6pm | admission 18 euro, children 10 euro | www.lajitaoasispark.com | on the FV 2 at La Lajita; there are also free buses from Morro Jable, Esquinzo,* Costa Calma, Caleta de Fustes and Corralejo, *information tel. 9 02 40 04 34*

The camel station across the road also belongs to the zoo. A INSIDER TIP swaying ride on a camel in a caravan is a lot of fun. 10 euro, children 5 euro.

HIKING FROM AJUY TO CALETA NEGRA
(124 B3) (*ᗰ C8*)

The short hike to the mysterious 'pirate caves' is an ideal outing for older children (from 8 years) the route is described in the 'The Centre' chapter under Pájara.

THE SOUTH

WALKS ON THE BEACH
(129 D6, E5) (*ᗰ A13–14*)

For older children, the beach hikes on the coast between Jandía Playa and the start of the lagoon, are a lot of fun. This section has lots of interesting rocky outcrops that divide the beach, the best time is during low tide early in the morning or in the early evening, when you can also do some bird watching.

Animal workforce at the outdoor museum La Alcogida

FESTIVALS & EVENTS

HOLIDAYS

1 Jan *New Year's Day;* **6 Jan** *Epiphany* (family festival where gifts are exchanged); **March/April** *Holy Thursday, Good Friday;* **1 May** *Labour Day;* **30 May** *Canaries Day; Corpus Christi;* **25 July** *St John's Day;* **15 Aug** *Assumption;* **12 Oct** *National Day (Discovery of the Americas);* **1 Nov** *All Saints' Day;* **6 Dec** *Constitution Day;* **8 Dec** *Feast of the Immaculate Conception;* **25 Dec** *Christmas Day,* mass at midnight. Christmas carols in *La Antigua* church *(Sat or Sun of the 4th Advent, approx. 5pm).*

FIESTAS

Every town celebrates its patron saint day with processions, children's festivals, church services, music and dancing.

21 JANUARY ▶ *Valle de Santa Inés*
2 FEBRUARY ▶ *Gran Tarajal*

FEBRUARY/MARCH
▶ ★ ● *Carnival:* The majority of events take place in **Puerto del Rosario** and the prelude is a masked ball. Further balls

follow, amongst them the ▶ *Verbena de la Sabana,* where the men wear wigs and dress in drag.

MARCH/APRIL
▶ *Semana Santa/Easter:* Processions in many towns with images of Mary and Christ.

MAY
▶ *Tefía (4th); Tarajalejo (8th); La Lajita (13th)*

MAY/JUNE
▶ *Corpus Christi.* In **Puerto del Rosario** with 'flower' carpets made from coloured stones.

JUNE
▶ *Lajares (13th); Ajuy (24th); Vallebrón (24th); Las Playitas (29th)*

JULY
▶ *Pájara (2nd); Casillas del Angel (26th)*

14 JULY
Betancuria: During the ▶ *Día de San Buenaventura* drummers and pipers celebrate the Castilian conquest of the island.

The fun only really begins at midnight when the numerous festivals start the festivities in honour of the local patron saints

16 JULY
▶ *Fiesta Nuestra Señora del Carmen* is celebrated in *Corralejo* and *Morro Jable* with a parade and ▶ ★ *boat procession.*

AUGUST
▶ *Tetir (4th); Tiscamanita (3rd Sun); Tindaya (15th); El Cotillo (approx. 22nd); Tefía (28th)*

SEPTEMBER
▶ *La Antigua (8th);* On the 3rd Friday night pilgrims cross the mountain to *Vega de Río de las Palmas,* where a shrine houses the Virgen de la Peña. The *Virgen de la Peña fiesta* then goes on for over 40 hours.

7 OCTOBER
La Oliva; Puerto del Rosario: The ▶ ★ *Fiesta Nuestra Señora del Rosario* is the largest fiesta on the island with elaborate costumes and music.

13 OCTOBER
▶ *Tuineje:* Festival of St Michael, INSIDER TIP historical spectacle about the battle of Tamacite and the victory over English pirates.

19 OCTOBER ▶ *La Ampuyenta*
30 NOVEMBER ▶ *Tetir*
8 DECEMBER ▶ *Betancuria*

EVENTS

Corralejo hosts an eight day ▶ *Blues-festival* during March and in May in the wrestling arena in La Antigua artisans present their crafts at ▶ ★ *Feria Insular de Artesanía* for a week.

The highlight of the year is the ▶ ● *Wind-surfing World Cup* in front of the lagoon of Playa Barca from mid-July.

During November people meet in Corralejo for the ▶ *International Kite Festival.*

LINKS, BLOGS, APPS & MORE

LINKS

▶ www.spiritoffuerteventura.com This is a local English online magazine that not only has up-to-date island news but also offers all sorts of information about the best places to visit, excursions, cocktail bars, weather, videos and much more

▶ www.fuerteonline.com/index-uk-2.htm Fuerteventura Travel Guide is an online portal with photographs, videos, vouchers and community news and online discussion group

▶ www.fuertenews.com Another English language online weekly magazine with news, classifieds and useful sections like 'Fun Stuff' and 'Island Information'

BLOGS

▶ www.alohasurfacademy.com/category/non-classe-en Blog by the owners of a surf school in Corralejo with entries about yoga retreats, surf classes, volcano hikes and island tours

▶ www.canarynightlife.net/forum An online open forum that discusses anything and everything about the bars, restaurants and nightlife on the island

▶ www.fuerteventura-forum.com Discussion groups with various categories and topics

▶ www.casadelaburra.WordPress.com A Spanish blog by the owner of a holiday home that details important cultural and tourist events on the island

▶ www.fuerteventurarelocation.co.uk This blog is geared to expats who want to make the move to Fuerteventura but it is also full of useful tourist tips and information like where to find the best tapas, the late night chemist and the best accommodation

Regardless of whether you are still preparing your trip or already in Fuerteventura: these addresses will provide you with more information, videos and networks to make your holiday even more enjoyable

VIDEOS

▶ vimeo.com/channels/Fuerte ventura A video site with about 27 posts of good quality videos

▶ www.rene-egli.co The island's top windsurfing centre has a video that gives you an excellent idea of what to expect on Fuerteventura

▶ www.youtube.com Type in Turismo de Fuerteventura for some of the island's official tourism videos

▶ www.responsibletravel.com/Fuerte ventura-Travel-Guide/Fuerteventura-Podcasts.htm A very interesting series of podcasts from island locals (in English) that are grouped into categories like 'Nature & Wildlife', 'Culture & History' and 'Food'

APPS

▶ Spain Tweets Spanish travel networking for iPhones

▶ Google Maps Navigation Useful navigation tool for smart and android phones and tablets

▶ iTranslate A free translation tool – type in a phrase and hear it translated back to you in Spanish – very handy when you need to order food or ask for directions

NETWORK

▶ www.ukawayfm.com Website for the English language radio station that broadcasts local and international news, weather reports and island events 24 hours a day

▶ www.airbnb.com A popular site for travellers who prefer to stay in accommodation offered by locals. The Feuerteventura site has a number of listings from beach duplex to a tiny Spanish *casa rural* with a walled garden. The site is constantly updated with new listings and user reviews

TRAVEL TIPS

ARRIVAL

There are a large number of budget and charter companies that offer direct flights from the UK to Fuerteventura. With such a selection it is simply a matter of comparing prices and hunting for the best deal. In the UK, Easyjet flies from Liverpool and Gatwick, Monarch Airlines flies from London, Manchester and Birmingham, Ryanair from Scotland and Thomas Airways from Newcastle. Most travel agents have very reasonable flat-rate package deals that include flight and accommodation. For those travelling from outside of the UK the best option would be to transfer at one of the major European airports like London or Madrid. Spain, France and the Netherlands also have direct flights on their national carriers. There are also frequent inter-island flights to the other Canary Islands. On arrival in Fuerteventura, the transport from the airport to the holiday destinations are usually included in the package. There are many car rental companies with counters at the airport. Their cars can then be found at the numbered parking spots on the right (northern) end of the airport parking lot.

Fuerteventura has no direct ferry connections. You have to change over: coming from Cadíz in Arrecife on Lanzarote (continue by ferry from Playa Blanca to Corralejo) or in Las Palmas (continue by ferry to Morro Jable). There is only a connection once a week and it takes about two nights and a day. For two people with a passenger car you can expect to pay about 1300 euro. Information and reservations for ferry passage at travel agents or directly at www.trasmediterranea.es or www.navieraarmas.com.

BANKS & CREDIT CARDS

During the week, banks are mostly open from 8.30am–2pm, Saturdays until 12.30 or 1pm. You can draw money from ATMs using a Visa card, MasterCard, EC and debit card.

Major credit cards are accepted by many banks, hotels, car rental companies as well as in shops and restaurants.

Some useful numbers to block credit cards are: Visa: *tel. 9 00 99 11 24*, Euro and MasterCard: *tel. 9 00 97 12 31*

BUSES

There are 17 bus lines that connect all the large towns. However, the lines most relevant to tourists are lines 1 and 10 (Morro Jable/Costa Calma–capital, mostly hourly),

RESPONSIBLE TRAVEL

It doesn't take a lot to be environmentally friendly whilst travelling. Don't just think about your carbon footprint whilst flying to and from your holiday destination but also about how you can protect nature and culture abroad. As a tourist it is especially important to respect nature, look out for local products, cycle instead of driving, save water and much more. If you would like to find out more about eco-tourism please visit: *www.ecotourism.org*

From arrival to weather

Holiday from start to finish: the most important addresses and information for your trip to Fuerteventura

line 3 (Caleta de Fuste–capital, mostly half-hourly), line 5 (Morro Jable–Costa Calma, mostly hourly), line 6 (Corralejo–capital, mostly half-hourly), line 7 (Cotillo–capital, three times daily), line 8 (Corralejo–Cotillo, mostly hourly) and line 25 (Morro Jable/Costa Calma–Oasis Park, mostly hourly). Lines 3 and 10 stop at the airport.

CAMPING

The official campsites have no amenities (toilets, showers, water, etc.) and to use them you are required to register in the town hall of the relevant community where you also need to pay a deposit. Maximum duration of stay is seven days.

CAR & CAR HIRE

An international license is not essential as national licenses are accepted. For more information about the traffic regulations see *www.fuerteventurarelocation. co.uk/driving-in-fuerteventura*. Buckling up is required by law and the speed limit for passenger cars in the towns is 50km/h and 90km/h on the country roads. The blood-alcohol limit is 0.25 and the Spanish police have zero tolerance. In Fuerteventura there are often roadblocks, especially at night and during weekends.

There is a wide choice of rental cars available in the holiday resorts and at the airport. Three day and weekend rates are the best. A small rental car starts at 160 euro per week, an off-road vehicle at about 60 euro per day. Ensure that unlimited mileage, collision damage waiver and full personal accident insurance are included in the price.

To hire a car the minimum age is 21 (at some companies it is 23). During the high season you will need to book in advance. You do not need an off-road vehicle for normal travel around the island, but if you want to drive on the byways and gravel roads an off-road vehicle is recommended, but remember that most of the time this is excluded from the accident insurance.

BUDGETING

Camel rides	£8/$13
	children £4/$6.50
Coffee	80p/$1.30
	for an espresso
Car hire	from £55/$90
	for three days
Windsurfing	£95/$155
	for a three day beginner's course
Petrol	65p/$1
	per litre
Island tour	£40/$65
	with bus and guide

CONSULATES & EMBASSIES

BRITISH CONSULATE IN FUERTEVENTURA

A British consular officer makes routine visits to Fuerteventura and is available for assistance and advice at: *Hotel Barcelo Corralejo Bay | Avenida Grandes Playas 12 | Corralejo | La Oliva | 35660 Fuerteventura | tel. +349 02 10 93 56 | ukinspain.fco.gov.uk/en*

AMERICAN CONSULAR AGENCY IN LAS PALMAS

Edificio ARCA | C. Los Martinez de Escobar 3 | 35007 Las Palmas | tel. +349 28 22 25 52 | madrid.usembassy.gov/citizen-services/offices/las-palmas.html

CURRENCY CONVERTER

£	€	€	£
1	1.20	1	0.85
3	3.60	3	2.55
5	6	5	4.25
13	15.60	13	11
40	48	40	34
75	90	75	64
120	144	120	100
250	300	250	210
500	600	500	425

$	€	€	$
1	0.75	1	1.30
3	2.30	3	3.90
5	3.80	5	6.50
13	10	13	17
40	30	40	50
75	55	75	97
120	90	120	155
250	185	250	325
500	370	500	650

For current exchange rates see www.xe.com

CUSTOMS

The Canaries is a free trade zone without customs control. UK citizens do not have to pay any duty on goods brought from another EU country as long as tax was included in the price and they are for private consumption. The limits are: 800 cigarettes, 400 cigarillo, 200 cigars, 1kg smoking tobacco, 10L spirits, 20L liqueurs, 90L wine, 110L beer. Travellers from the USA, Canada, Australia or other non-EU countries are allowed to enter with the following tax-free amounts: 200 cigarettes or 100 cigarillos or 50 cigars or 250g smoking tobacco. 2L wine and spirits with less 22 vol % alcohol, 1L spirits with more than 22vol % alcohol content. Travellers to the United States who are returning residents of the country do not have to pay duty on articles purchased overseas up to the value of $800, but there are limits on the amount of alcoholic beverages and tobacco products. For the regulations for international travel for US residents please see *http://www.cbp.gov*

CYCLING

A word of warning: there are hardly any bicycle paths on the island, many roads are narrow and the local drivers have very little regard cyclists. Outside of the towns, helmets are compulsory and the alcohol limit also applies to cyclists.

ELECTRICITY

200 Volts. Adapters are needed for UK appliances.

EMERGENCY SERVICES

Dial *112* for the police, ambulance and fire brigade. Or contact your hotel for help.

FERRIES

Two ferry lines offer trips from Corralejo to Lanzarote/Playa Blanca daily, up to 14 trips (travelling time 25 minutes, price per trip from 23 euro, car transport from 29 euro). *Líneas Fred Olsen | tel. 9 02 10 01 07 | www.fredolsen.es; Naviera Armas | tel. 9 02 45 65 00 | www.navieraarmas.com*

A car ferry from the Naviera Armas line travels daily from Morro Jable to Las Palmas de Gran Canaris (travel time 3 hours), once weekly further to Tenerife. Additional connections to Gran Canaria from Puerto del Rosario (3×/week) and from Gran Tarajal (2×/week).

FLIGHT CONNECTIONS

There are almost 16 daily flight connections to Las Palmas from Gran Canaria and six to Tenerife/Los Rodeos, more often during the week to Madrid. No connections to other Canary Islands. Bookings and information: *Binter (tel. 9 02 39 13 92 | www.binternet.com)* also *Islas Airways (tel. 9 02 47 74 78 | www.islasairways.com)*. More flight information *tel. airport 9 02 40 47 04*.

HEALTH

Holidaymakers with a European Health Insurance Card (EHIC) issued by your social-security office will be treated free of charge in casualty wards and hospitals associated with the Spanish *Seguridad Social*. In other cases, you should make sure that you receive a detailed receipt for any treatment received to be able to claim a refund when you return home.

DOCTORS

For a list of English speaking doctors see: *http://ukinspain.fco.gov.uk/en/about-us/ other-locations/las-palmas-consulate/ local-contacts* and download 'Doctors in Fuerteventur' pdf.

CHEMISTS

Farmacías can be found in all the large holiday resorts in Exquinzo, Puerto del Rosario and Gran Tarajal. Chemists are usually open from 9am–1pm and 4pm–7pm Mon–Fri and 9am–1pm Sat. The sign *Farmacia de Guardia* lets you know where the nearest 24-hour chemist is.

IMMIGRATION

Citizens of the UK and Ireland, USA, Canada, Australia and New Zealand need only a valid passport to enter all EU countries. Children under the age of 12 need a children's passport.

INFORMATION

For online information and to order brochures see: *www.spain.info/en_GB/*

FUERTEVENTURA

Patronato de Turismo | C. Almirante Lallermand 1 (opposite the mill) | Puerto del Rosario | tel. +34 9 28 53 08 44 | www. fuerteventuraturismo.com

SPANISH TOURIST BOARD OFFICES

– *6th floor | 64 North Row | London | W1K 7DE | tel. 020 73 17 20 11 | www.spain. info/en_GB/*
– *60 East 42nd Street | suite 53000 53rd floor | New York | tel. +1 21 22 65 88 22 | www.spain.info/en_US/*

INTERNET

There are some helpful sites on the internet like *www.fuerteventura.com*, *www. sunnyfuerteventura.com* or *www.fuerte venturainfo.com* where you can find information about accommodation, maps, island news and readers' forums. Look at live webcams at *www.meteosurfcanarias. com/webcams*.

INTERNET CAFÉS

Internet cafés are available in all the large holiday resorts. Here are a few of them:

CALETA DE FUSTE *at the Slow Boat II Chinese restaurant | on the northern side opposite the childrens' playground*

CORRALEJO *Whereabouts? Apartamentos Hoplaco, local 2*

COSTA CALMA *Cyber Connection | in the CC El Palmeral (near the petrol station)*

MORRO JABLE/JANDÍA PLAYA *Internet-café Jandía, in the basement of CC Cosmo*

OPENING HOURS

Shops are open during the week between 9am–1pm and 5pm–8pm, in the holiday season they often also stay open on weekends.

PHONE & MOBILE PHONE

There are numerous pay phones on the island. When calling abroad it is cheaper to call from telephone shops *(locutorios)* or with *teletarjetas* (cards with a personal identification number) available from 6 euro which can be used with most telephones except for the older public telephones.

Now that the European Union has capped the roaming prices within the EU, it does not matter which Spanish mobile network you use. If you travel to Spain often or make a lot of calls to Spain, it would be worthwhile to get a Spanish SIM card which will cut costs even further. *Dialling code to the UK: 0044, to the US: 001; to Spain: 0034. Your mobile phone will automatically choose a Spanish network.*

POST

There are post offices in Corralejo, Costa Calma, Gran Tarajal and Morro Jable

(Mon–Sat noon) as well as in Puerto del Rosario (Mon–Fri 8.30am–8.30pm | Sat 9.30am–1pm). Stamps are usually also available at hotel reception, these stamps are from private postal companies so do not post your mail in the usual public letterboxes but hand them in at the same place where you purchased the stamps.

PRICES

Prices on Fuerteventura are generally on par with those in the rest of Europe. A simple lunch in the most affordable restaurant is about 7 to 8 euro while a restaurant dinner will set you back 15 to 25 euro. There are no fees to access any of the beaches but you will need to pay if you want the use of deckchairs and umbrellas. Alcohol, tobacco and petrol are cheaper than at home.

SMOKING

Spanish legislature has banned smoking in restaurants unless they have a separate smoking room. Many hosts use a legal loophole by simply claiming that the whole restaurant is the designated smoking area. The restaurants usually have signs at the entrance. *Prohibido fumar* = non-smoking and *Permitido fumar* or *Fumadores* = smoking allowed.

TAXI

The basic rate on weekdays 6am–10pm is 2.68 euro and 0.47 euro is added per kilometre; evenings and holidays 3.21 euro plus 0.58 euro per kilometre.

TIPPING

To tip waiters and taxi drivers, you can round up the bill by 5–10 per cent. For chambermaids 3 euro is recommended at the beginning and thereafter every four to five days depending on how happy you are with the service. For other services, small tips are also customary.

TIME

Fuerteventura has GMT all year round (simultaneous switching to winter or summer time). The North American east coast is 5 hours behind, the west coast 8 hours.

WATER

Drinking water is sold everywhere in plastic bottles or canisters. Although the tap water is safe, you are advised not to drink it.

WHEN TO GO & WHAT TO WEAR

Fuerteventura's season is year-round. However, the temperatures are most pleasant in spring and autumn. During mid-summer, the sun and constant strong winds can be unpleasant for those with a sensitive nature and small children (swirling sand on the beach!). From January to April it can be cool and the water temperatures are too cold to swim. The main season prices usually apply to July/August and Christmas. During August, many restaurants close for the summer holidays. Always take along a jacket as well as a jersey during the winter and spring as the evenings can be chilly.

WEATHER IN FUERTEVENTURA

	Jan	Feb	March	April	May	June	July	Aug	Sept	Oct	Nov	Dec
Daytime temperatures in °C/°F	19/66	19/66	20/68	21/70	23/73	24/75	27/81	27/81	26/79	24/75	21/70	19/66
Nighttime temperatures in °C/°F	12/54	12/54	13/55	13/55	15/59	16/61	18/64	19/66	18/64	17/63	15/59	13/55
Sunshine hours/day	6	7	8	8	9	9	10	10	8	7	6	6
Precipitation days/month	3	2	1	1	1	0	0	0	0	1	3	3
Water temperatures in °C/°F	1/64	18/64	17/63	17/63	18/64	20/68	20/68	21/70	22/72	22/72	20/68	19/66

USEFUL PHRASES SPANISH

PRONUNCIATION

c	before 'e' and 'i' like 'th' in 'thin'
ch	as in English
g	before 'e' and 'i' like the 'ch' in Scottish 'loch'
gue, gui	like 'get', 'give'
que, qui	the 'u' is not spoken, i.e. 'ke', 'ki'
j	always like the 'ch' in Scottish 'loch'
ll	like 'lli' in 'million'; some speak it like 'y' in 'yet'
ñ	'nj'
z	like 'th' in 'thin'

IN BRIEF

Yes/No/Maybe	sí/no/quizás
Please/Thank you	por favor/gracias
Hello!/Goodbye!/See you	¡Hola!/¡Adiós!/¡Hasta luego!
Good morning!/afternoon!/ evening!/night!	¡Buenos días!/¡Buenos días!/¡Buenas tardes!/¡Buenas noches!
Excuse me, please!	¡Perdona!/¡Perdone!
May I ...?/Pardon?	¿Puedo ...?/¿Cómo dice?
My name is ...	Me llamo ...
What's your name?	¿Cómo se llama usted?/¿Cómo te llamas?
I'm from ...	Soy de ...
I would like to .../Have you got ...?	Querría .../¿Tiene usted ...?
How much is ...?	¿Cuánto cuesta ...?
I (don't) like that	Esto (no) me gusta.
good/bad/broken/doesn't work	bien/mal/roto/no funciona
too much/much/little/all/nothing	demasiado/mucho/poco/todo/nada
Help!/Attention!/Caution!	¡Socorro!/¡Atención!/¡Cuidado!
ambulance/police/fire brigade	ambulancia/policía/bomberos
May I take a photo here	¿Podría fotografiar aquí?

DATE & TIME

Monday/Tuesday/Wednesday	lunes/martes/miércoles
Thursday/Friday/Saturday	jueves/viernes/sábado
Sunday/working day/holiday	domingo/laborable/festivo
today/tomorrow/yesterday	hoy/mañana/ayer

¿Hablas español?

"Do you speak Spanish?" This guide will help you to say the basic words and phrases in Spanish

hour/minute/second/moment	hora/minuto/segundo/momento
day/night/week/month/year	día/noche/semana/mes/año
now/immediately/before/after	ahora/enseguida/antes/después
What time is it?	¿Qué hora es?
It's three o'clock/It's half past three	Son las tres/Son las tres y media
a quarter to four/a quarter past four	cuatro menos cuarto/ cuatro y cuarto

TRAVEL

open/closed/opening times	abierto/cerrado/horario
entrance/exit	entrada/acceso salida
departure/arrival	salida/llegada
toilets/ladies/gentlemen	aseos/señoras/caballeros
free/occupied	libre/ocupado
(not) drinking water	agua (no) potable
Where is ...?/Where are ...?	¿Dónde está ...? /¿Dónde están ...?
left/right	izquierda/derecha
straight ahead/back	recto/atrás
close/far	cerca/lejos
traffic lights/corner/crossing	semáforo/esquina/cruce
bus/tram/U-underground/	autobús/tranvía/metro/
taxi/cab	taxi
bus stop/cab stand	parada/parada de taxis
parking lot/parking garage	parking/garaje
street map/map	plano de la ciudad/mapa
train station/harbour/airport	estación/puerto/aeropuerto
ferry/quay	transbordador/muelle
schedule/ticket/supplement	horario/billete/suplemento
single/return	sencillo/ida y vuelta
train/track/platform	tren/vía/andén
delay/strike	retraso/huelga
I would like to rent ...	Querría ... alquilar
a car/a bicycle/a boat	un coche/una bicicleta/un barco
petrol/gas station	gasolinera
petrol/gas / diesel	gasolina/diesel
breakdown/repair shop	avería/taller

FOOD & DRINK

Could you please book a table for tonight for four?	Resérvenos, por favor, una mesa para cuatro personas para hoy por la noche.
on the terrace/by the window	en la terraza/junto a la ventana

The menu, please/	¡El menú, por favor!
Could I please have ...?	¿Podría traerme ... por favor?
bottle/carafe/glass	botella/jarra/vaso
knife/fork/spoon	cuchillo/tenedor/cuchara
salt/pepper/sugar	sal/pimienta/azúcar
vinegar/oil/milk/cream/lemon	vinagre/aceite/leche/limón
cold/too salty/not cooked	frío/demasiado salado/sin hacer
with/without ice/sparkling	con/sin hielo/gas
vegetarian/allergy	vegetariano/vegetariana/alergía
May I have the bill, please?	Querría pagar, por favor
bill/receipt/tip	cuenta/recibo/propina

SHOPPING

pharmacy/chemist	farmacia/droguería
baker/market	panadería/mercado
butcher/fishmonger	carnicería/pescadería
shopping centre/department store	centro comercial/grandes almacenes
shop/supermarket/kiosk	tienda/supermercado/quiosco
100 grammes/1 kilo	cien gramos/un kilo
expensive/cheap/price/more/less	caro/barato/precio/más/menos
organically grown	de cultivo ecológico

ACCOMMODATION

I have booked a room	He reservado una habitación.
Do you have any ... left?	¿Tiene todavía ...?
single room/double room	habitación individual/habitación doble
breakfast/half board/	desayuno/media pensión/
full board (American plan)	pensión completa
at the front/seafront/garden view	hacia delante/hacia el mar/hacia el jardín
shower/sit-down bath	ducha/baño
balcony/terrace	balcón/terraza
key/room card	llave/tarjeta
luggage/suitcase/bag	equipaje/maleta/bolso
swimming pool/spa/sauna	piscina/spa/sauna
soap/toilet paper/nappy (diaper)	jabón/papel higiénico/pañal
cot/high chair/nappy changing	cuna/trona/cambiar los pañales
deposit	anticipo/caución

BANKS, MONEY & CREDIT CARDS

bank/ATM/	banco/cajero automático/
pin code	número secreto
cash/credit card	en efectivo/tarjeta de crédito
bill/coin/change	billete/moneda/cambio

HEALTH

doctor/dentist/paediatrician	médico/dentista/pediatra
hospital/emergency clinic	hospital/urgencias
fever/pain/inflamed/injured	fiebre/dolor/inflamado/herido
diarrhoea/nausea/sunburn	diarrea/náusea/quemadura de sol
plaster/bandage/ointment/cream	tirita/vendaje/pomada/crema
pain reliever/tablet/suppository	calmante/comprimido/supositorio

POST, TELECOMMUNICATIONS & MEDIA

stamp/letter/postcard	sello/carta/postal
I need a landline phone card/	Necesito una tarjeta telefónica/
I'm looking for a prepaid card for my mobile	Busco una tarjeta prepago para mi móvil
Where can I find internet access?	¿Dónde encuentro un acceso a internet?
dial/connection/engaged	marcar/conexión/ocupado
socket/adapter/charger	enchufe/adaptador/cargador
computer/battery/	ordenador/batería/
rechargeable battery	batería recargable
e-mail address/at sign (@)	(dirección de) correo electrónico/arroba
internet address (URL)	dirección de internet
internet connection/wifi	conexión a internet/wifi
e-mail/file/print	archivo/imprimir

LEISURE, SPORTS & BEACH

beach/sunshade/lounger	playa/sombrilla/tumbona
low tide/high tide/current	marea baja/marea alta/corriente

NUMBERS

0	cero	14	catorce
1	un, uno, una	15	quince
2	dos	16	dieciséis
3	tres	17	diecisiete
4	cuatro	18	dieciocho
5	cinco	19	diecinueve
6	seis	20	veinte
7	siete	100	cien, ciento
8	ocho	200	doscientos, doscientas
9	nueve	1000	mil
10	diez	2000	dos mil
11	once	10 000	diez mil
12	doce	1/2	medio
13	trece	1/4	un cuarto

NOTES

MARCO POLO TRAVEL GUIDES

ALGARVE
AMSTERDAM
ATHENS
AUSTRALIA
BANGKOK
BARCELONA
BERLIN
BRAZIL
BRUSSELS
BUDAPEST
BULGARIA
CALIFORNIA
CAMBODIA
CAPE TOWN
  WINE LANDS,
  GARDEN ROUTE
CAPE VERDE
CHINA
COLOGNE
COPENHAGEN
CORFU
COSTA BLANCA
  VALENCIA
COSTA DEL SOL
  GRANADA
CRETE
CUBA
CYPRUS
  NORTH AND
  SOUTH
DUBAI
DUBLIN
DUBROVNIK &
  DALMATIAN
  COAST
EDINBURGH
EGYPT
EGYPT'S RED
  SEA RESORTS
FINLAND
FLORENCE

FLORIDA
FRENCH ATLANTIC
  COAST
FRENCH RIVIERA
  NICE, CANNES &
  MONACO
FUERTEVENTURA
GRAN CANARIA
GREECE
HONG KONG
  MACAU
ICELAND
INDIA
INDIA SOUTH
  GOA & KERALA
IRELAND
ISRAEL
ISTANBUL
JORDAN
KOS
KRAKOW
LAKE GARDA
LANZAROTE
LAS VEGAS
LISBON

LONDON
LOS ANGELES
MADEIRA
  PORTO SANTO
MADRID
MALLORCA
MALTA
  GOZO
MAURITIUS
MILAN
MOROCCO
MUNICH
NAPLES &
  THE AMALFI COAST
NEW YORK
NEW ZEALAND
NORWAY
OSLO
PARIS
PHUKET
PORTUGAL
PRAGUE
RHODES

ROME
SAN FRANCISCO
SARDINIA
SCOTLAND
SEYCHELLES
SHANGHAI
SICILY
SINGAPORE
SOUTH AFRICA
STOCKHOLM
TENERIFE
THAILAND
TURKEY
TURKEY
  SOUTH COAST
TUSCANY
UNITED ARAB
  EMIRATES
USA SOUTHWEST
VENICE
VIENNA
VIETNAM

- PACKED WITH INSIDER TIPS
- BEST WALKS AND TOURS
- FULL-COLOUR PULL-OUT MAP
  AND STREET ATLAS

ROAD ATLAS

The green line ▬▬ indicates the Trips & Tours (p. 90–95)
The blue line ▬▬ indicates The perfect route (p. 30–31)

All tours are also marked on the pull-out map

Photo: beach promenade in Morro Jable

Exploring Fuerteventura

The map on the back cover shows how the area has been sub-divided

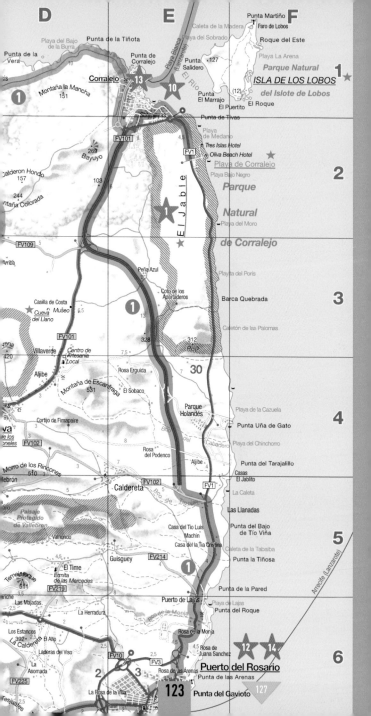

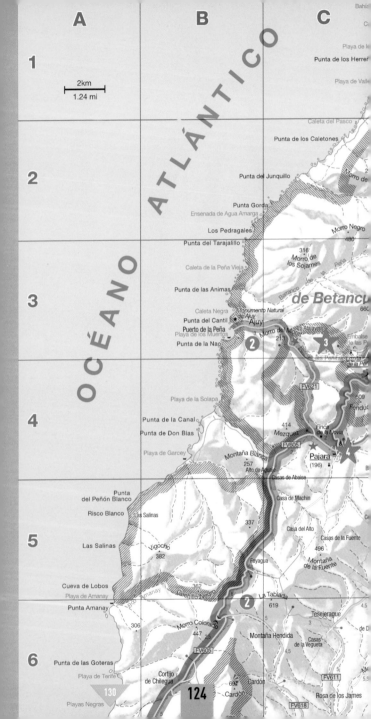

Bahía

Playa de l...
Punta de los Herrer...

Playa de Valle...

Caleta del Pasco
Punta de los Caletones

Punta del Junquillo
Morro de...

Punta Gorda
Ensenada de Agua Amarga
Los Pedregales
Morro Negro

Punta del Tarajalillo
480

Caleta de la Peña Vieja
316
Morro de
los Sojames
Peña

Punta de las Animas
660
Barranco
de Betancu...

Caleta Negra Monumento Natural
de Ajuy
Punta del Cantil Ajuy
Puerto de la Peña Morro del Moral La Atalayeja
Playa de los Muertos 213 Embalse
Punta de la Nao de las P...
Las Peñitas Ermita de
la Pe...

FV621
5
609
Fendú...

Playa de la Solapa

Punta de la Canal 414 Finca
Mezquez de la Novia
Punta de Don Blas FV605
Pajara
Playa de Garcey Montaña Blanca (196)
257 B...
Alto de Aguije
Casas de Abaise

Punta
del Peñón Blanco Casa de Machin

Risco Blanco Las Salinas
337 Casa del Alto
Casas de la Fuente
496
Las Salinas Vigocho Montaña
382 de la Fuente
Feyagua

Cueva de Lobos 362
Playa de Amanay Barranco de Amanay Cuchillo Negro La Tablada 4.5
Punta Amanay 2 619 Tesejerague
306 de Di...
Morro Colorado
447 Montaña Hendida Casas
de la Vegueta
Punta de las Goteras FV605
Playa de Tenife Cortijo 69... FV611
130 de Chilegua Cardón
124 Cardón Rosa de los James
Playas Negras FV618

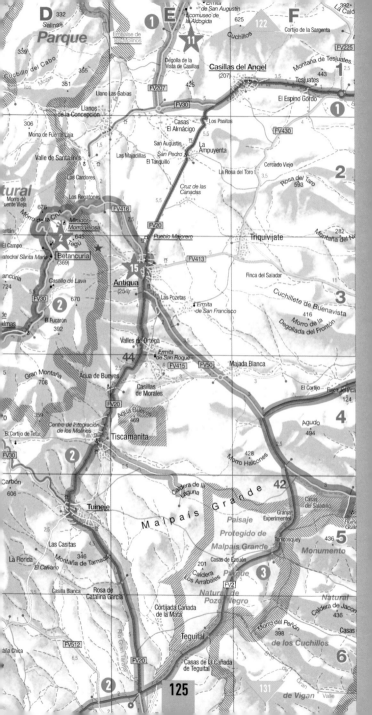

Parque

D 332 Salinas

339

Cucbillo del Cabo

351 355

306

Morro de Fuente Laja

Valle de Santa Inés

Los Cardores

tural

Morro de Fuente Vieja 676

Morro de la Cruz

antán

El Campo

atedral Santa María 645 Tegú

Betancuria (369)

ancuría 724

Castillo de Lava

FV30 2 670

de almas 5

El Fucarón 392

5 Gran Montaña 708 359

o

FV30

Carbón 606

Las Casitas

La Florida

El Calvario

Casilla Blanca

aña Chica

FV512 6,5

Enlace de los Molinos

Ecomuseo de la Alcogida

E **1** F

625 **122** Cuchillos

Cortijo de la Sargenta

FV225

Ermita de San Augustín

Degollada de la Vista de Casillas

Llano Las Gabias

FV207

Casillas del Angel (207)

425 5

Montaña de Tesjuates 443 Tesjuates

3,5 El Espino Gordo

1

1

Llanos de la Concepción

FV30

Casas El Almácigo Los Pasitos

FV430

San Augustín 5,5

Las Majadillas San Pedro El Tanquillo

La Ampuyenta

Cercado Viejo

La Rosa del Toro 3,5

Rosa del Taro 593

2

FV416 2,5

Mirador Morro Velosa

Los Regatones

Cruz de las Canadas 5,5

FV20

Pueblo Majorero

Triquivijate

Montaña del N 282

11

15

Antigua (254)

FV413

Finca del Saladar

Cuchillete de Buenavista

416 Morro de la Degollada del Frontón

3

Las Pozetas

Ermita de San Francisco

Valles de Ortega

44 Ermita de San Roque

FV415 FV50 **Majada Blanca**

El Cortijo Finca del Vica 124

4

Aqua de Bueyes

FV20

Casillas de Morales

Aqua Bueyes 469

3

Agudo 494

Centro de Integración de los Molinos

El Cortijo de Tetur

FV30

2

Tiscamanita

5,5

428 Morro Halcones

42

2,5

M a l p a í s   G r a n d e

Caldera de la Laguna

Casas del Saladillo

Ruin Guai

Tuineje

2,5

Montaña de Tamacita 346

Rosa de Catalina García

201

Paisaje Protegido de **Malpaís Grande**

Granja Experimental

Toncosquey 436

5

Monumento

Casas de Erduén

Caldera Los Arrabales

Parque

FV2

3

Natural de **Pozo Negro**

Natural

Caldera de Jacon 436

Casas

6

Cortijada Cañada de la Mata

Rio Gran Tarajal

4,5

Morro del Peñón 398

de los Cuchillos

Tequital

Casas de la Cañada de Tequital

FV20

2

125

131

de Vigan Valle

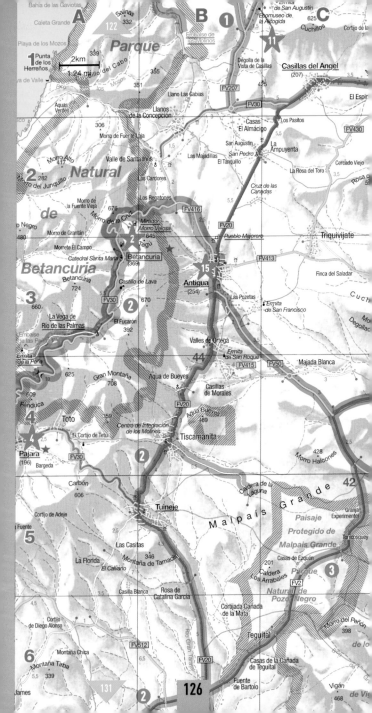

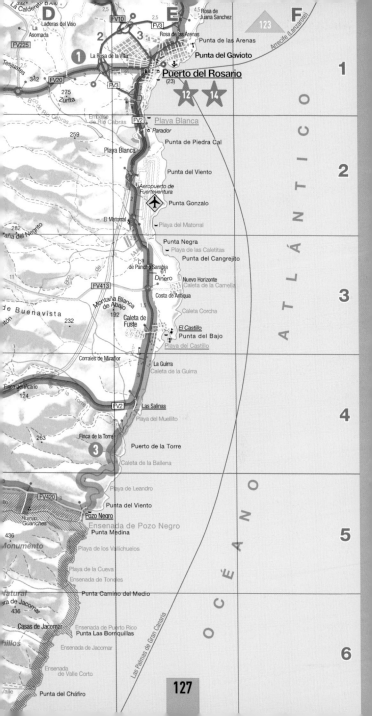

Map Labels

D | **E** | **F**

La Caldereta Brava
Laderas del Viso
La Asomada
FV10
2.5
FV3
Rosa de Juana Sanchez
4.5
123
Arrecife (Lanzarote)

2
3
Rosa de las Arenas
Punta de las Arenas
Punta del Gavioto

FV225
Tesjuates
2.5
La Rosa de la Vila
1
Puerto del Rosario
(23)

342
FV20
275
Zurita
FV3
12
14
O

B Co de Rio Cabras
259
Embalse de Rio Cabras
FV2
Playa Blanca
Parador
T

Playa Blanca
Punta de Piedra Cal
L

282
ña del Negro
Punta del Viento
Á

Aeropuerto de Fuerteventura
Punta Gonzalo
N

El Matorral
Playa del Matorral
T

11
Punta Negra
Playa de las Caletitas
Punta del Cangrejito
Í

de Buenavista
232
Ca de Pancho Sarabia
Dinero
Nuevo Horizonte
Caleta de la Camella
Costa de Antigua
C

FV413
Montaña Blanca de Abajo
192
Caleta Corcha
O

Caleta de Fuste
El Castillo
Punta del Bajo
Playa del Castillo

Corrales de Miraflor
La Guirra
Caleta de la Guirra

Fnca del Vicario
124
FV2
Las Salinas
Playa del Muellito
4

263
Finca de la Torre
3
Puerto de la Torre
Caleta de la Ballena

Playa de Leandro
FV420
Punta del Viento
O

Ruinas Guanches
Pozo Negro
Ensenada de Pozo Negro
Punta Medina
C

436
Monumento
Playa de los Vallichuelos
É

Natural ra de Jacomar
436
Playa de la Cueva
Ensenada de Tonelas
Punta Camino del Medio
A

Casas de Jacomar
Punta Las Borriquillas
Ensenada de Puerto Rico
N

hillos
Ensenada de Jacomar
O

Ensenada de Valle Corto
Las Palmas de Gran Canaria

/alle
Punta del Cháfiro

ATLÁNTICO

OCÉANO

A   B   C

1

2km
1.24 mi

2

3

O C É A N O   A T L

4

Playa c

EL ISLOTE

★ Playa de Cofete

Punta Pesebre

**Punta de
Mal Rayo**   Punta de Barlovento
Caleta de la   Roque del Moro
Madera

5
Punta Cotillo
o de Cachorros
Las Talahijas   189   Cofete

Casa y Manantial   Fraile
del Mosquito   683   486   de Jar

Janc
80

3

Playa de Ojos   ★ **7**   **M**   424   Casas
**Punta
del
Tigre**   **3**   Las Pilas   de Gran Valle

390
Cueva de la Negra   **a**   Cuchillo del Palo   441   Morro Munguía   **d**   **e**
Punta Salinas   La Rajila   **c**   **i**   **z**   **o**
**Puerto
de la Cruz**   Playa de las Pilas
Playa de Juan Gómez   Casas de Joros
Punta de Jandía   Punta del Viento
6   Santa Cruz de Tenerife
Las Palmas de Gran Canaria   Puerto de la   Morro Jable
Cebaba   (27)

128

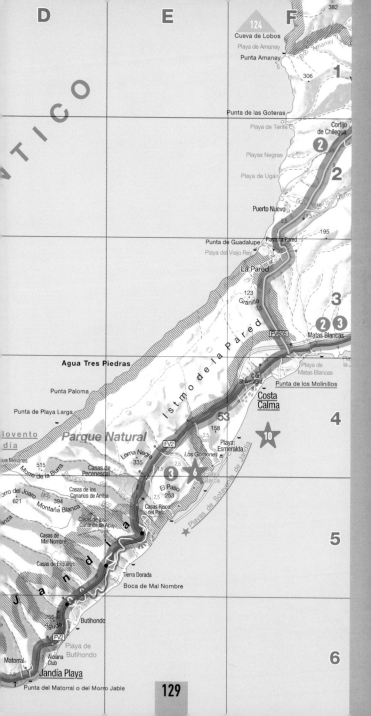

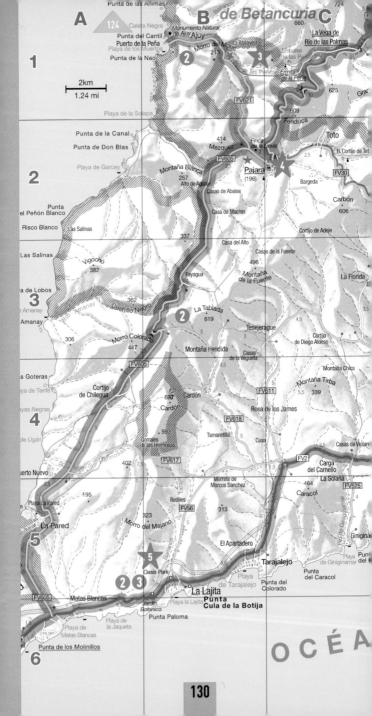

KEY TO ROAD ATLAS

Motorway · Toll		Autobahn · Gebührenpflichtige
junction · Toll station ·	Trento	Anschlussstelle · Gebührenstelle ·
Junction with number ·		Anschlussstelle mit Nummer ·
Motel · Restaurant · Snackbar ·		Rasthaus mit Übernachtung ·
Filling-station ·		Raststätte · Kleinraststätte ·
Parking place with and without WC		Tankstelle · Parkplatz mit und ohne WC
Motorway under construction and	Datum .... Date	Autobahn in Bau und geplant mit
projected with completion date		Datum der Verkehrsübergabe
Dual carriageway (4 lanes)		Zweibahnige Straße (4-spurig)
Trunk road ·	14 .... E45	Fernverkehrsstraße ·
Road numbers		Straßennummern
Important main road		Wichtige Hauptstraße
Main road · Tunnel · Bridge	)=:=(	Hauptstraße · Tunnel · Brücke
Minor roads		Nebenstraßen
Track · Footpath		Fahrweg · Fußweg
Tourist footpath (selection)		Wanderweg (Auswahl)
Main line railway		Eisenbahn mit Fernverkehr
Rack-railway, funicular		Zahnradbahn, Standseilbahn
Aerial cableway · Chair-lift		Kabinenschwebebahn · Sessellift
Car ferry · Passenger ferry		Autofähre · Personenfähre
Shipping route		Schifffahrtslinie
Nature reserve · Prohibited area		Naturschutzgebiet · Sperrgebiet
National park, natural park · Forest		Nationalpark, Naturpark · Wald
Road closed to motor vehicles	X—X—X	Straße für Kfz. gesperrt
Toll road		Straße mit Gebühr
Road closed in winter	XII–II	Straße mit Wintersperre
Road closed or not recommended		Straße für Wohnanhänger gesperrt
for caravans		bzw. nicht empfehlenswert
Tourist route · Pass	Weinstraße 1510	Touristenstraße · Pass
Scenic view · Panoramic view ·		Schöner Ausblick · Rundblick ·
Route with beautiful scenery		Landschaftl. bes. schöne Strecke
Spa · Swimming pool	⚓	Heilbad · Schwimmbad
Youth hostel · Camping site	△	Jugendherberge · Campingplatz
Golf-course · Ski jump	⌁	Golfplatz · Sprungschanze
Church · Chapel	⌘	Kirche im Ort, freistehend · Kapelle
Monastery · Monastery ruin		Kloster · Klosterruine
Synagogue · Mosque	✡	Synagoge · Moschee
Palace, castle · Ruin		Schloss, Burg · Schloss-, Burgruine
Tower · Radio-, TV-tower		Turm · Funk-, Fernsehturm
Lighthouse · Power station		Leuchtturm · Kraftwerk
Waterfall · Lock		Wasserfall · Schleuse
Important building · Market place, area	▪	Bauwerk · Marktplatz, Areal
Arch. excavation, ruins · Mine	∴	Ausgrabungs- u. Ruinenstätte · Bergwerk
Dolmen · Menhir · Nuraghe	π	Dolmen · Menhir · Nuraghen
Cairn · Military cemetery	☆	Hünen-, Hügelgrab · Soldatenfriedhof
Hotel, inn, refuge · Cave		Hotel, Gasthaus, Berghütte · Höhle

Culture / Kultur

Picturesque town · Elevation	WIEN (171)	Malerisches Ortsbild · Ortshöhe
Worth a journey	★★ MILANO	Eine Reise wert
Worth a detour	★ TEMPLIN	Lohnt einen Umweg
Worth seeing	Andermatt	Sehenswert

Landscape / Landschaft

Worth a journey	★★ Las Cañadas	Eine Reise wert
Worth a detour	★ Texel	Lohnt einen Umweg
Worth seeing	Dikti	Sehenswert

Excursions & tours		Ausflüge & Touren
Perfect route		Perfekte Route
MARCO POLO Highlight	★1	MARCO POLO Highlight

INDEX

This index lists all sights, museums, and destinations, plus the names of important people and key words featured in this guide. Numbers in bold indicate a main entry.

WRITE TO US

e-mail: info@marcopologuides.co.uk

Did you have a great holiday?
Is there something on your mind?
Whatever it is, let us know!
Whether you want to praise, alert us
to errors or give us a personal tip –
MARCO POLO would be pleased to
hear from you.
We do everything we can to provide the
very latest information for your trip.

Nevertheless, despite all of our authors'
thorough research, errors can creep in.
MARCO POLO does not accept any
liability for this. Please contact us by
e-mail or post.

MARCO POLO Travel Publishing Ltd
Pinewood, Chineham Business Park
Crockford Lane, Chineham
Basingstoke, Hampshire RG24 8AL
United Kingdom

PICTURE CREDITS
Cover photograph: Playas de Sotavento, surfer on the coast (DuMont Bildarchiv: Lumma)
O. Baumli (26 left); Casa de la Burra: Marta Cabrera Hernández (17 top); DuMont Bildarchiv: Lumma (1 top, 2 top, 5, 30 top, 86, 89, 106 top); Widmann (front flap left, front flap right, 12, 41, 65, 104/105), Zaglitsch (2 centre top, 6, 18/19, 27, 49, 64, 78/79); Huber: Ripani (59), Schmid (24/25, 37, 56, 77, 106 bottom); ©istockphoto.com: Christian Martínez Kempin (17 bottom), naphtalina (16 bottom), webphotographeer (16 top); C. Lachenmaier (2 centre bottom, 2 bottom, 3 bottom 32/33, 34, 54/55, 68, 85, 92, 96/97); Laif: Hemispheres (94/95), Hilger (67, 98), Kuerschner (28); Look: age fotostock (10/11, 15, 29, 72, 107, 133), Frei (60), Limberger (82), Richter (3 centre, 7, 23, 44, 46, 50, 53, 90/91, 104, 120/121); mauritius images: AGE (20, 78), Habel (43); mauritius images/imagebroker: Eisele-Hein (9, 30 bottom), Moxter (100/101), Siepmann (8, 26 right, 28/29, 63), Tack (38), 68images (41); D. Renckhoff (102, 103, 105); Hans-Wilm Schütte (1 bottom); K. Simon (88); Skeleton Sea (16 centre); vario images: imagebroker (3 top, 70/71, 81); E. Wrba (74)

1st Edition 2013
Worldwide Distribution: Marco Polo Travel Publishing Ltd, Pinewood, Chineham Business Park, Crockford Lane, Chineham, Basingstoke, Hampshire RG24 8AL, United Kingdom. Email: sales@marcopolouk.com
© MAIRDUMONT GmbH & Co. KG, Ostfildern
Chief editor: Marion Zorn
Author: Hans-Wilm Schütte; editor: Jochen Schürmann
Programme supervision: Ann-Katrin Kutzner, Nikolai Michaelis, Silwen Randebrock
Picture editors: Barbara Schmid, Gabriele Forst
What's hot: wunder media, Munich
Cartography road atlas & pull-out map: © MAIRDUMONT, Ostfildern
Design: milchhof : atelier, Berlin; Front cover, pull-out map cover, page 1: factor product munich
Translated from German by Wendy Barrow; editor of the English edition: Margaret Howie, fullproof.co.za
Prepress: M. Feuerstein, Wigel
Phrase book in cooperation with Ernst Klett Sprachen GmbH, Stuttgart, Editorial by Pons Wörterbücher

DOS & DON'TS

Save yourself some trouble by taking note of the following

DO AVOID SWIMMING ON THE WEST COAST

Except for a few bays that are protected by reefs, the current along the west coast can be very strong and dangerous, especially if you lose your footing. Hardly a year goes by without someone being reckless.

DON'T RISK GETTING SUNBURNT

Or even heat stroke which can be very serious! A long walk on the first day of your summer holiday (even when it is overcast) could give you a nasty sunburn. This also applies to other times of the year when cool winds can make you forget just how powerful the sun's rays are. Always wear sun screen with a high protection factor – even when it is overcast – and stay out of the sun at midday. Small children and people with sensitive skin are most at risk.

DON'T BUY CAMERAS, ELECTRONIC GOODS OR WATCHES

There have been numerous reports of customers being cheated so you should exercise extreme caution. You should first check what the goods would cost at home and then also make sure that all the accessories are included. The safest approach to this issue is to simply avoid these items.

DO AVOID THE TEMPTATION TO DRIVE CROSS-COUNTRY

Of course it is tempting to take your vehicle off-road but you should definitely not do so in any of the nature parks like the Jandía peninsula or in the dunes of Corralejo. It is a crime and if caught you will liable for a hefty fine. And you will be driving without insurance and should something happen you will have to pay for any damages yourself.

DON'T OPT FOR AN 'ALL INCLUSIVE' PACKAGE

If you book 'all inclusive' you will be left to the devices of the organiser. What do you do if the salad is limp, the coffee is always cold and the vegetables are overcooked? What if you would have preferred some more diversity in the menu? Avoid this and book a holiday that allows you some freedom of choice by only paying for what you will need. Your holiday will not necessarily be more expensive and it will certainly be far better.

DO REMEMBER THE SIESTA

Fuertaventura, like the rest of Spain, observes the siesta and this means that a lot of the restaurants and shops will be closed for a few hours in the middle of the day.